PEN CONTROL
AND PRE-HANDWRITING PRACTICE
ACTIVITY BOOK
FOR KIDS

THIS BOOK BELONGS TO

NOTE: We recommend using a pencil or crayon ONLY.
If using marker pens or wet mediums, you may experience
color bleeding through to the next page.

To join our mailing list and see other titles available

Website: www.captaintimpublishing.com
Email: info@captaintimpublishing.com

 # STANDING LINES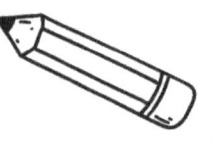
Trace the dotted standing lines.
Help the bee find the flower.

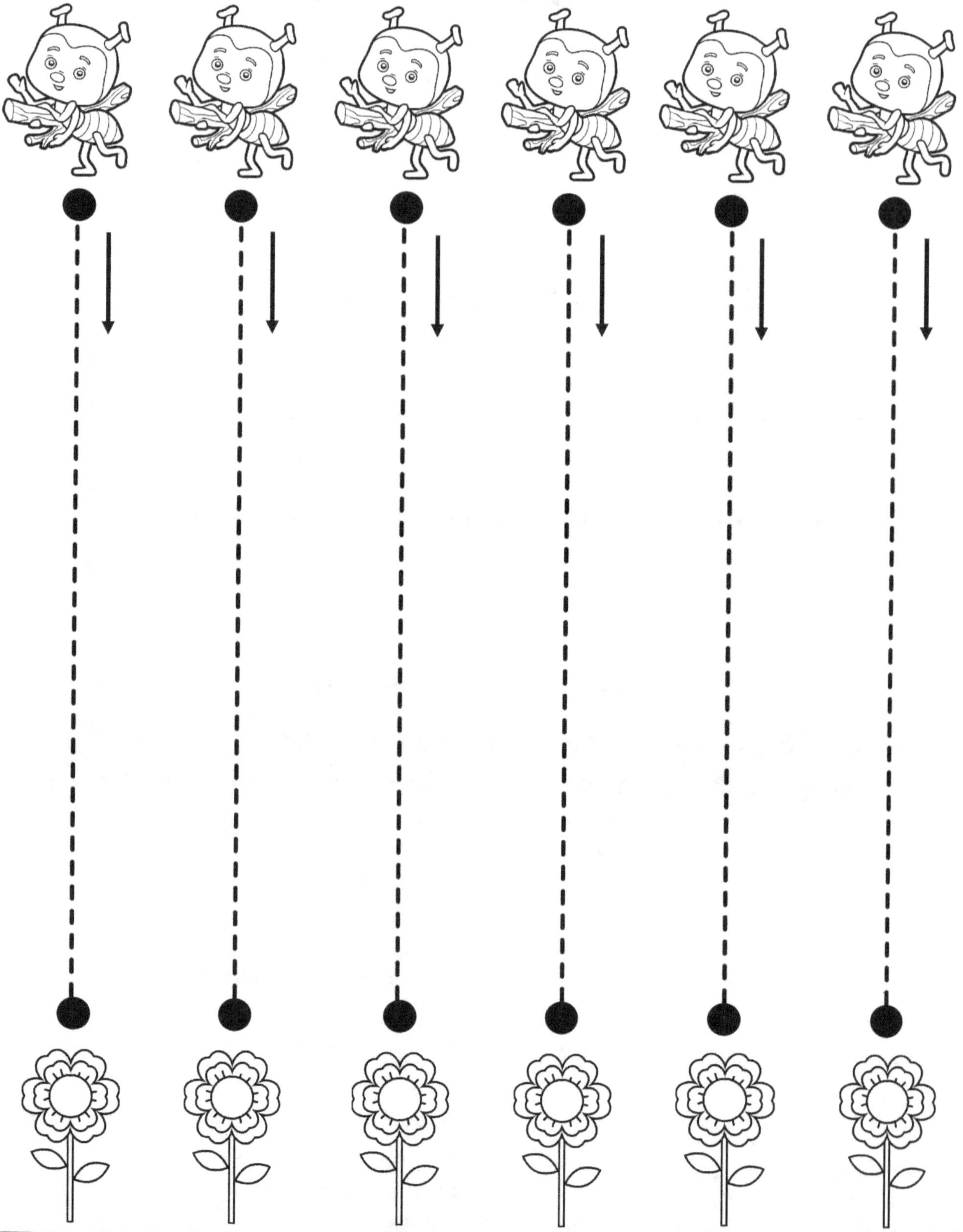

 # STANDING LINES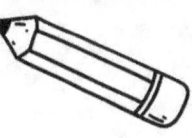
Trace the dotted standing lines.

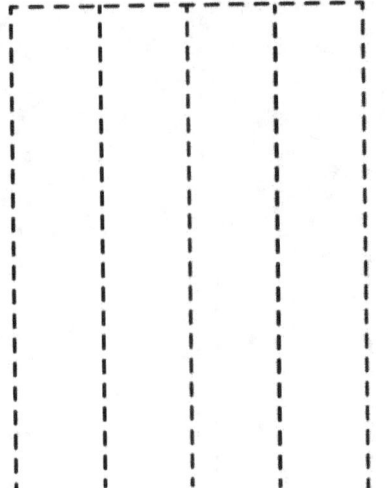
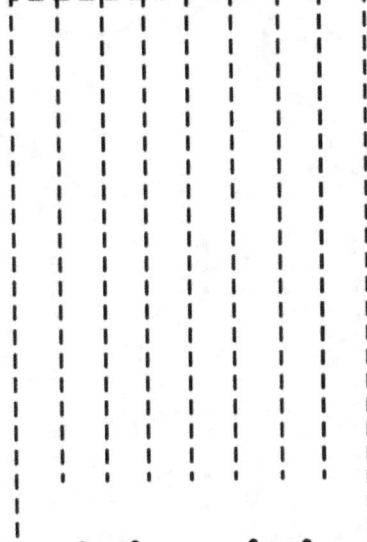

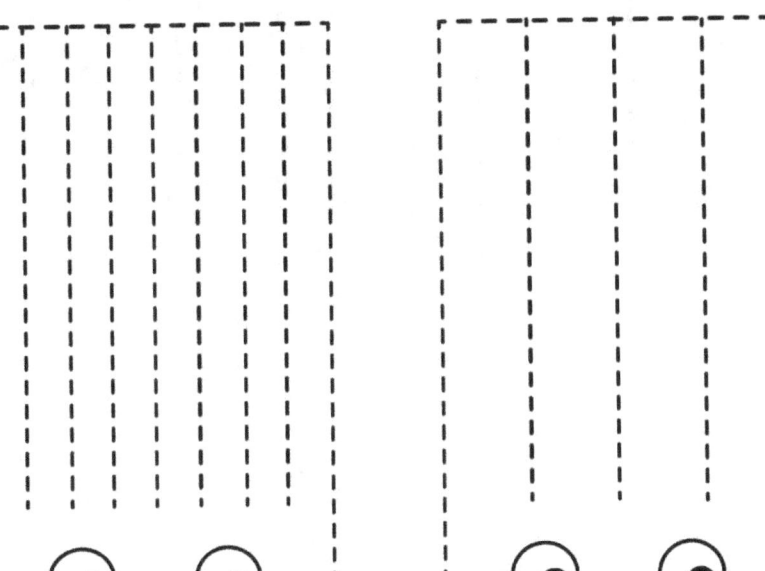
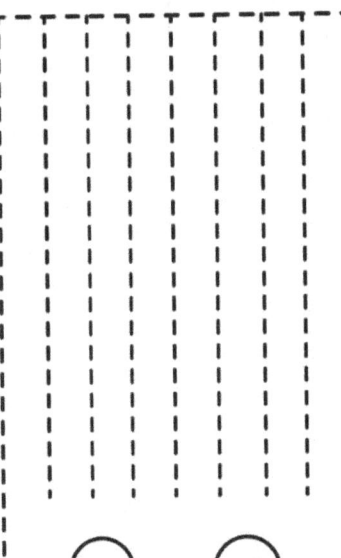

 # STANDING LINES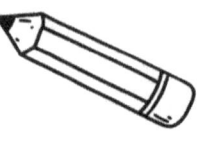

Trace the dotted standing lines.
Help water the plants.

 # STANDING LINES

Trace the dotted standing lines.
Help the rocket reach the star.

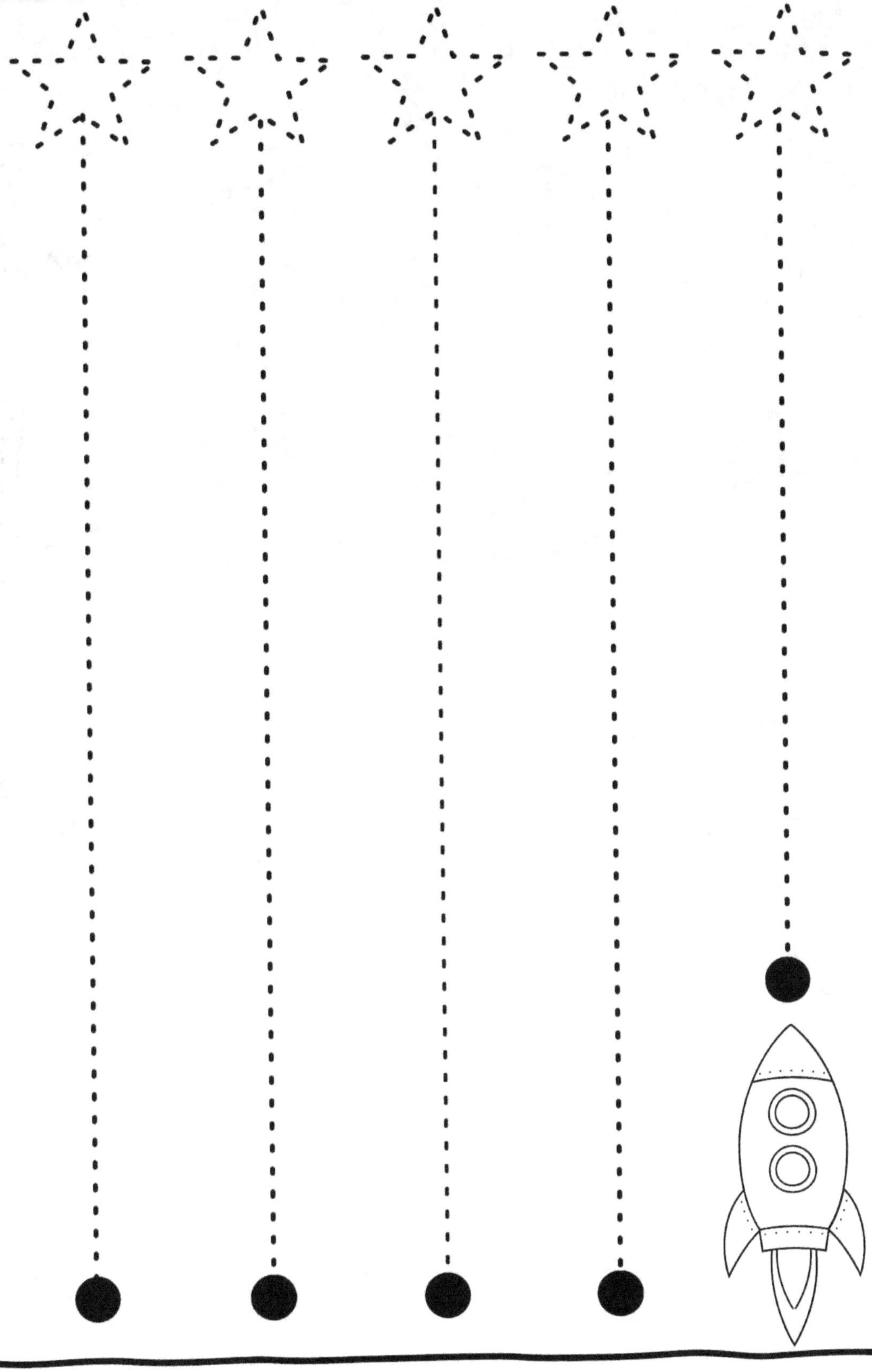

ZIGZAG LINES

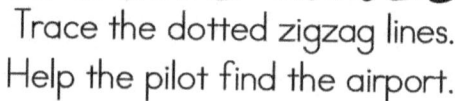

Trace the dotted zigzag lines.
Help the pilot find the airport.

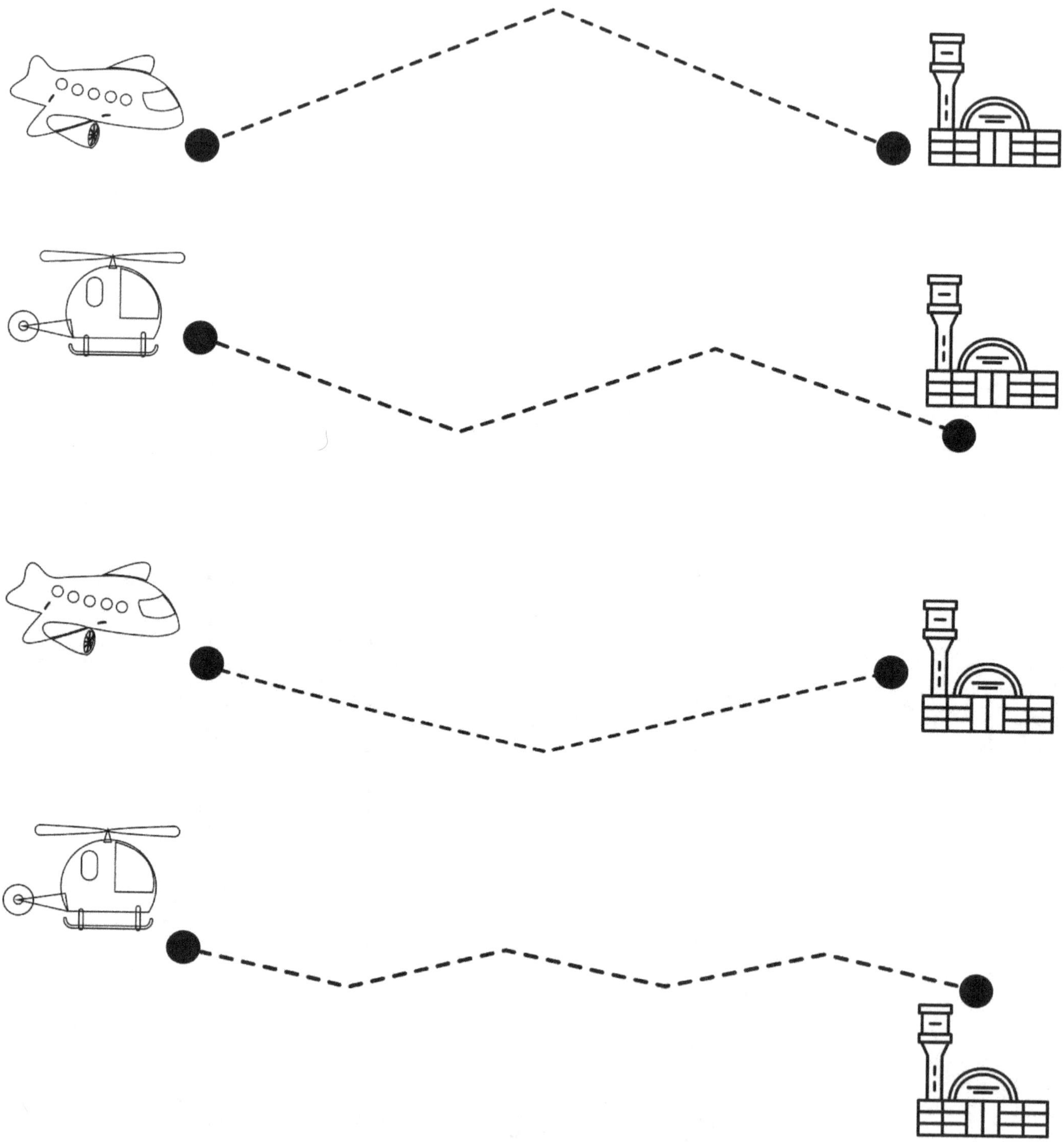

 # ZIGZAG LINES
Trace the dotted zigzag lines.
Help the dog find the bone.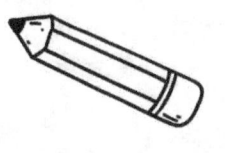

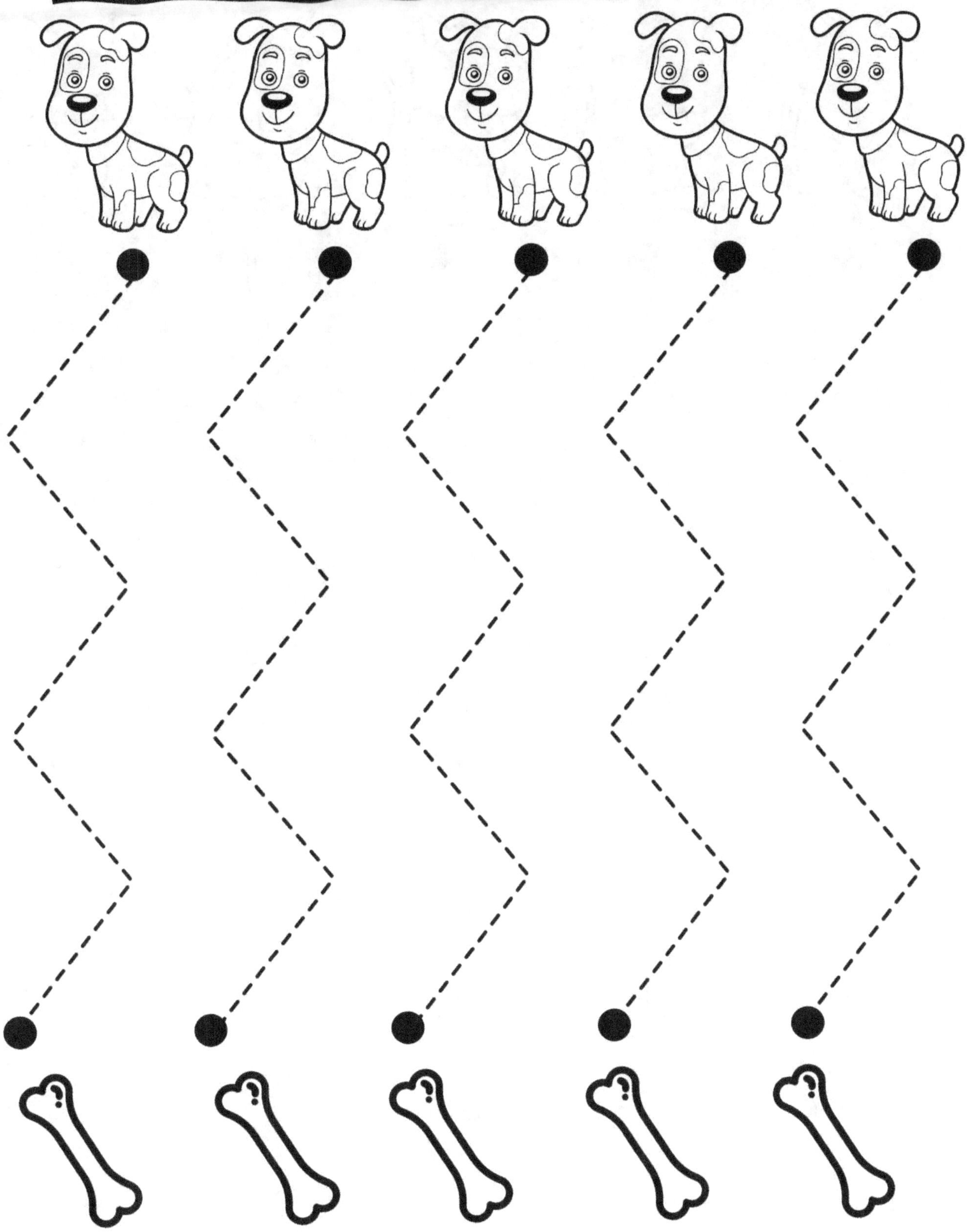

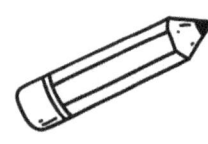 # ZIGZAG LINES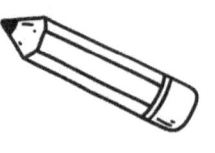

Trace the dotted zigzag lines.
Help the squirrel find the acorn.

 # ZIGZAG LINES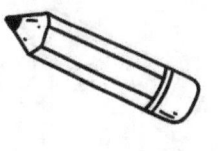

Trace the dotted zigzag lines.
Help the bee find the honey.

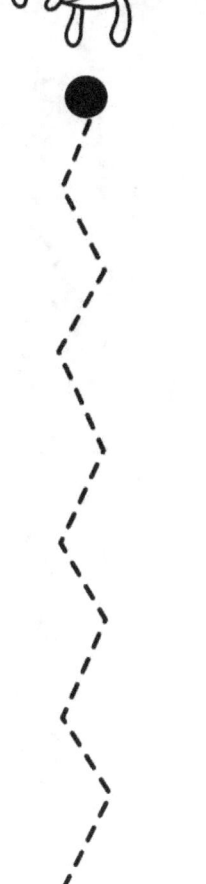 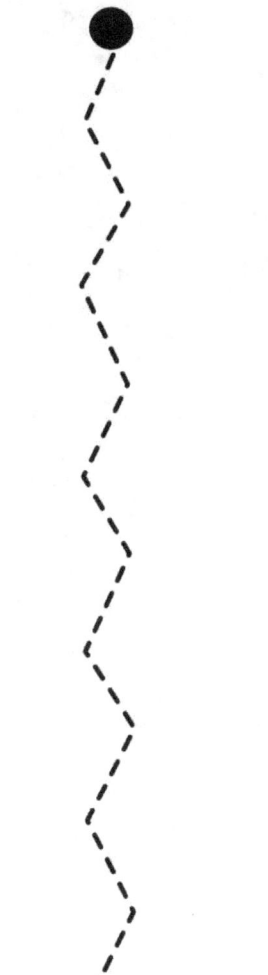 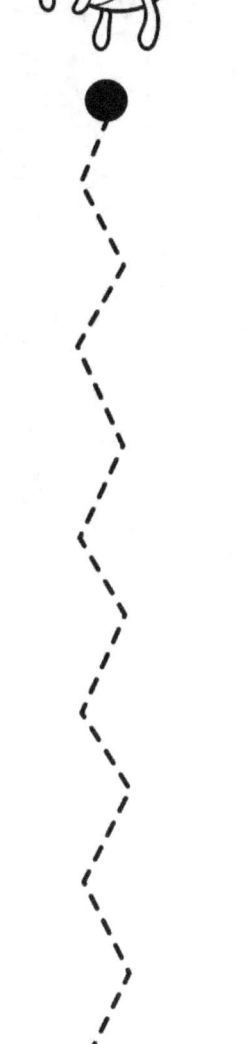 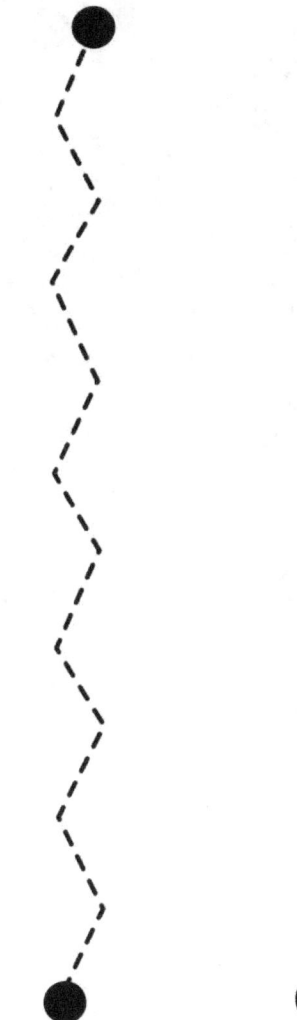 

ZIGZAG LINES

Trace the dotted zigzag lines.
Help the crab find the shell.

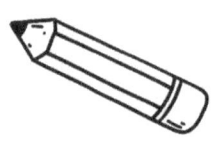

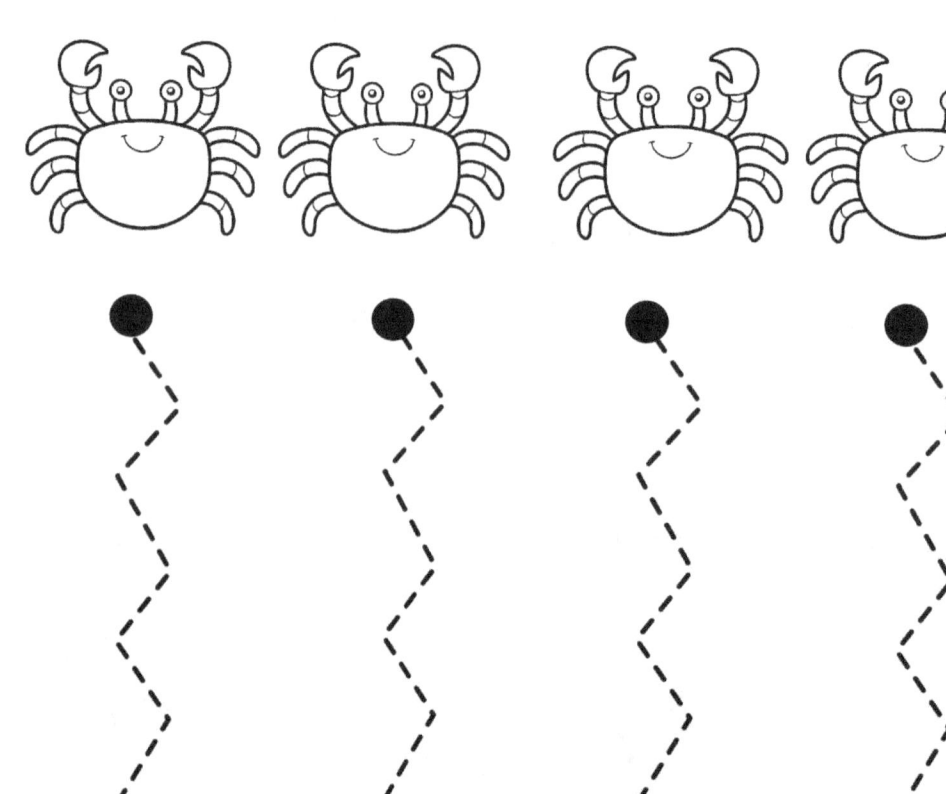

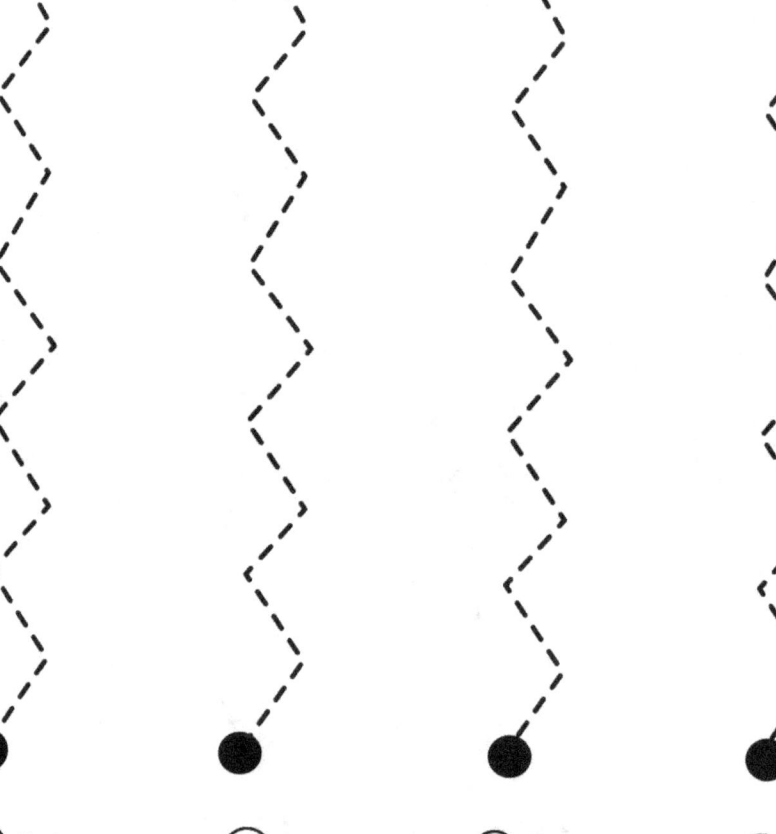

 # ZIGZAG LINES
Trace the dotted zigzag lines.

TRACE THE DOTTED LINE

Help the astronaut find the rocket.

SLEEPING LINES

Trace the dotted sleeping lines
and color the picture.

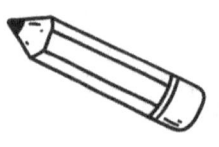

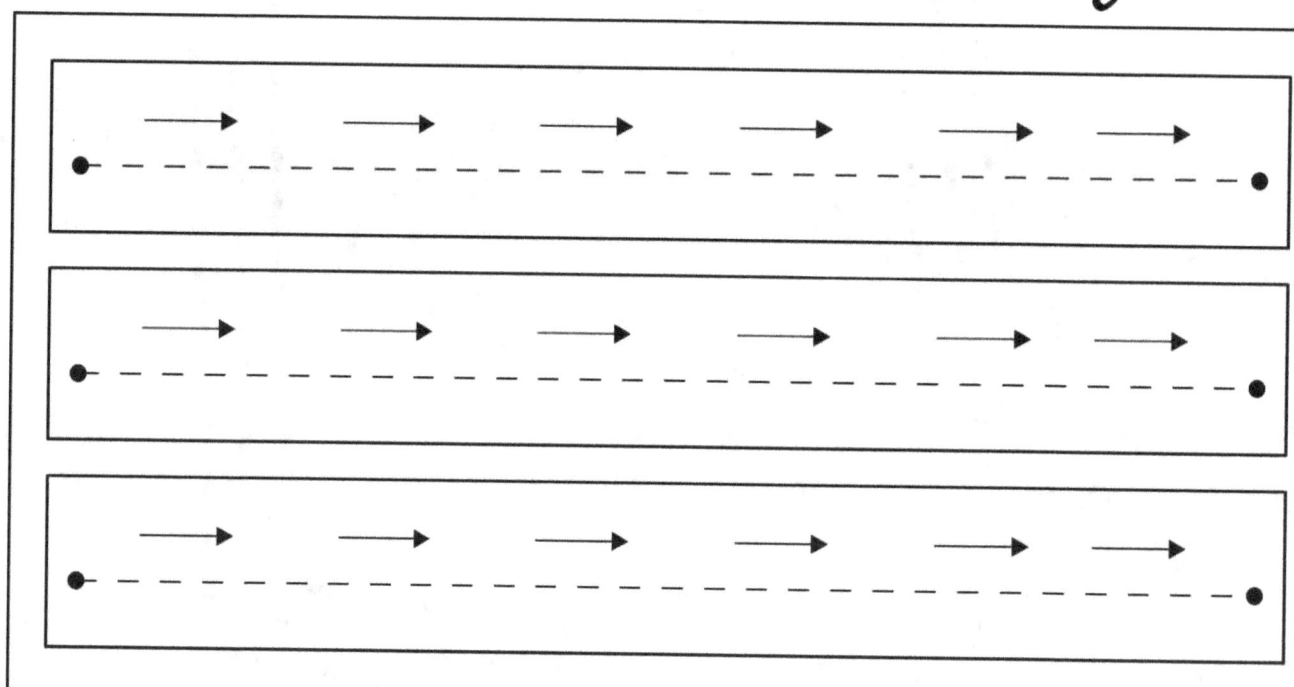

 # SLEEPING LINES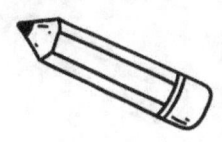
Trace the dotted sleeping lines.
Help the worm on it's travels.

 # SLEEPING LINES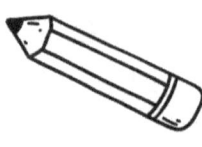

Trace the dotted sleeping lines.
Help the monkey find the banana.

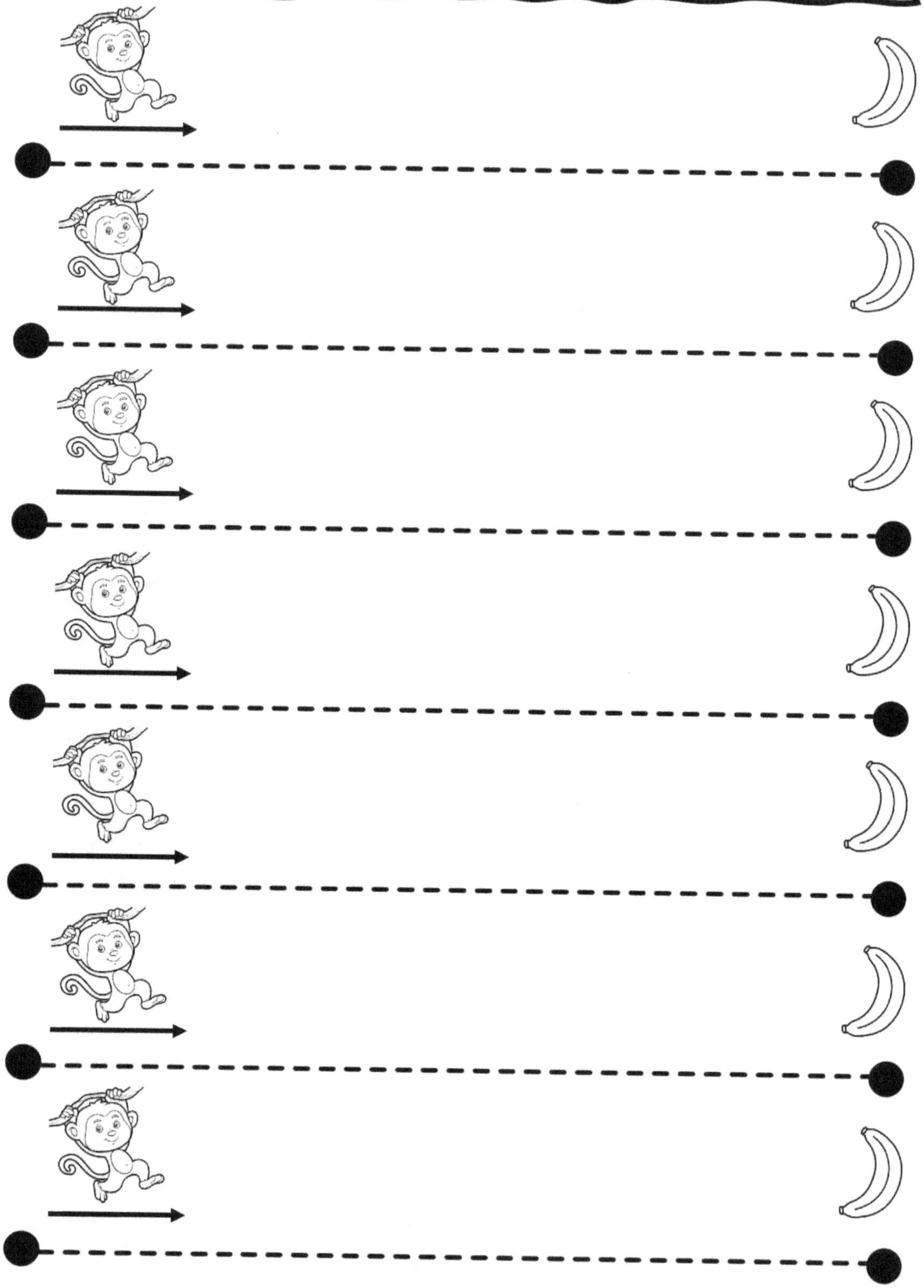

 # SLEEPING LINES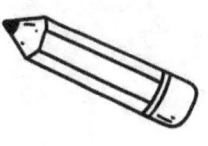

Trace the dotted sleeping lines.
Help the iguana find the tree.

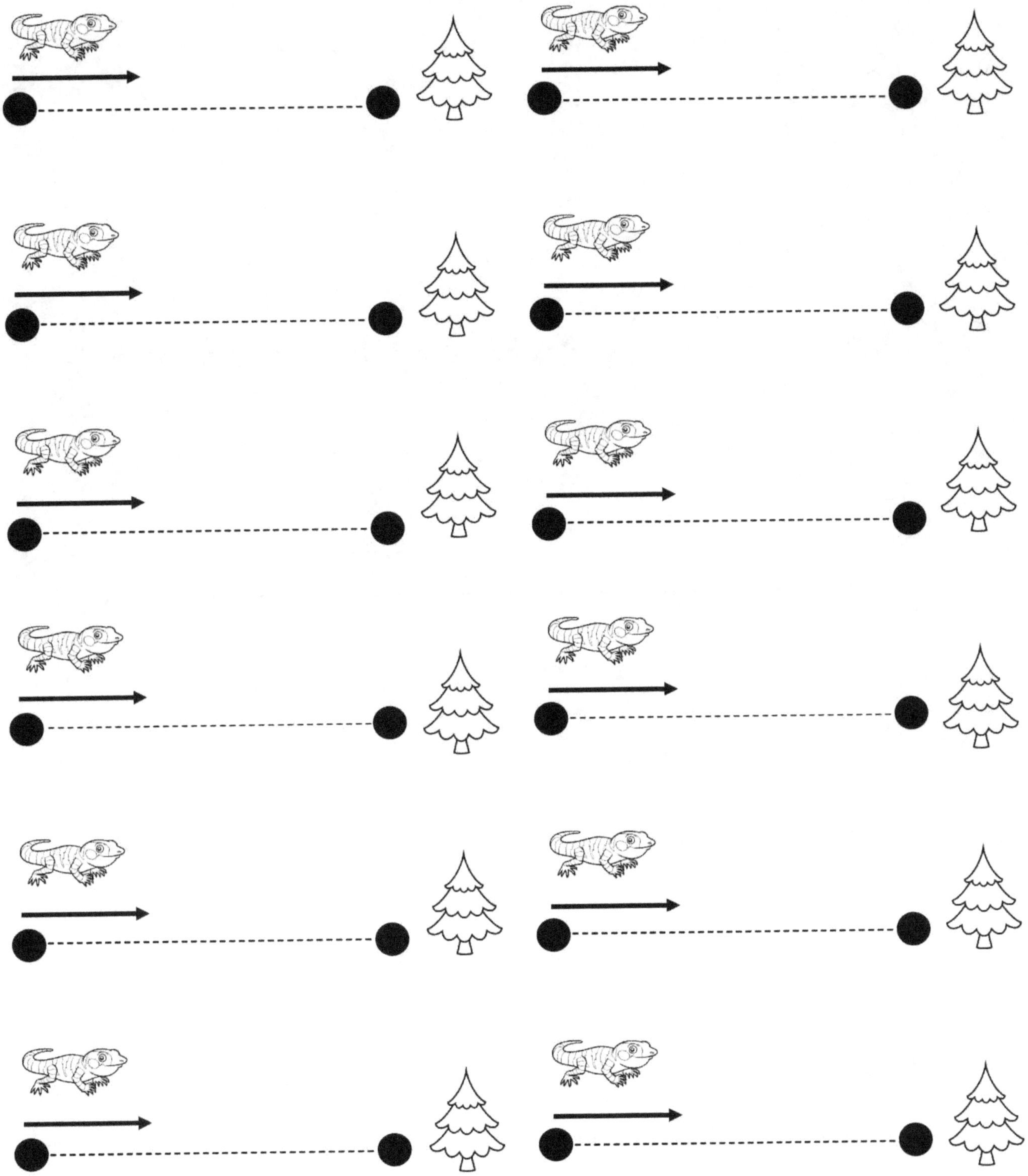

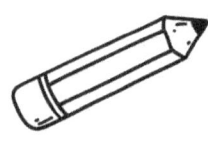

SLEEPING LINES

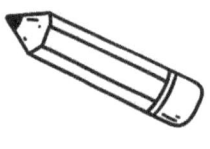

Trace the dotted sleeping lines.
Help each dinosaur reach their egg.

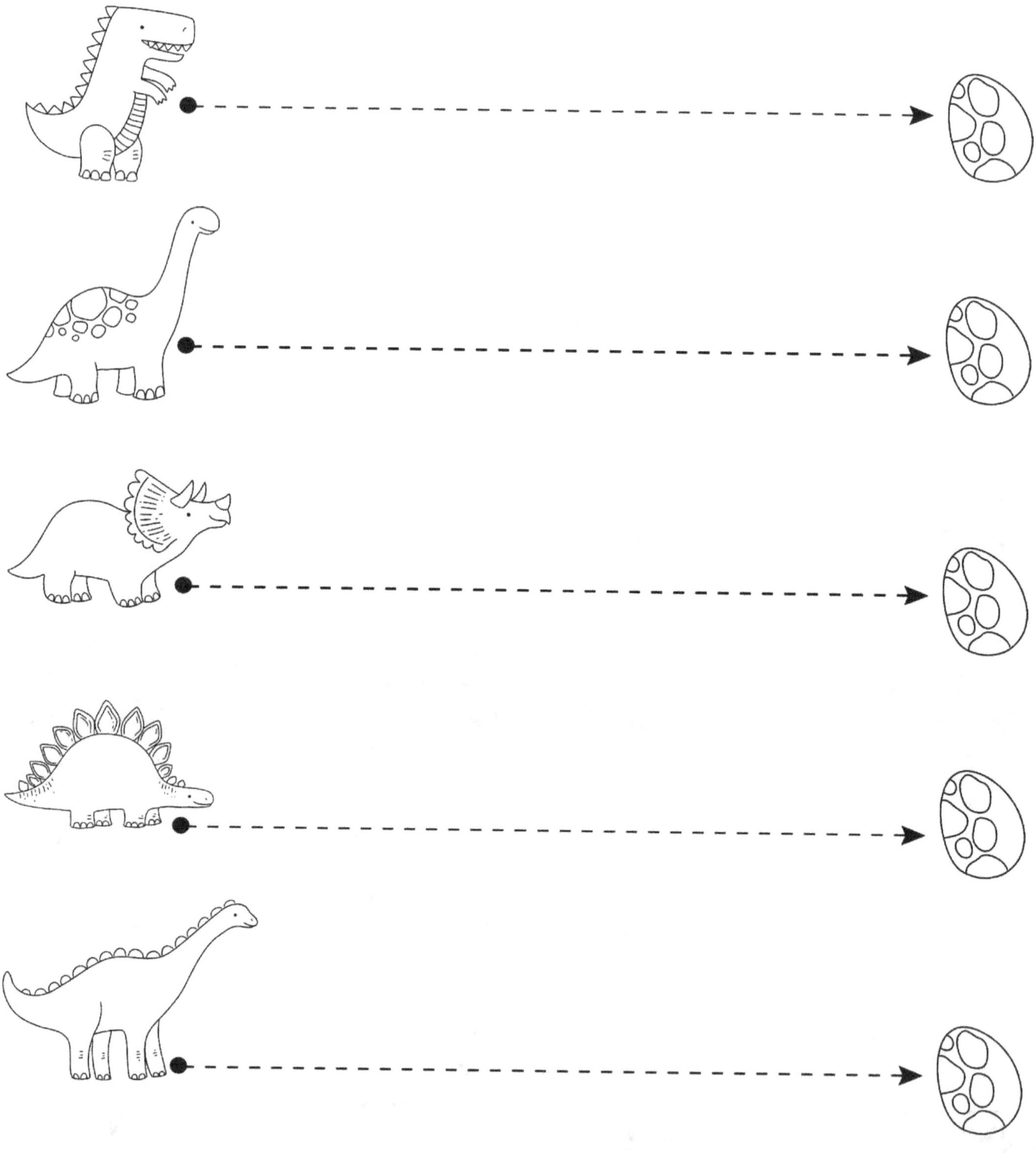

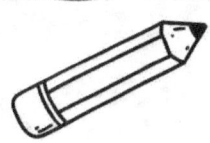 # SLEEPING LINES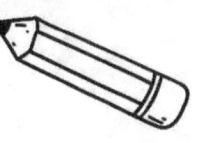
Trace the sleeping lines to
complete the picture and color it.

 # SLEEPING LINES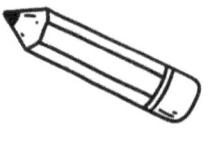
Trace the sleeping lines to
complete the picture and color it.

CASTLE LINES
Trace the castle dotted lines.

 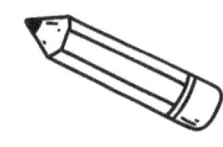

CASTLE LINES

Trace the castle dotted lines.
Help the vehicle reach it's destination.

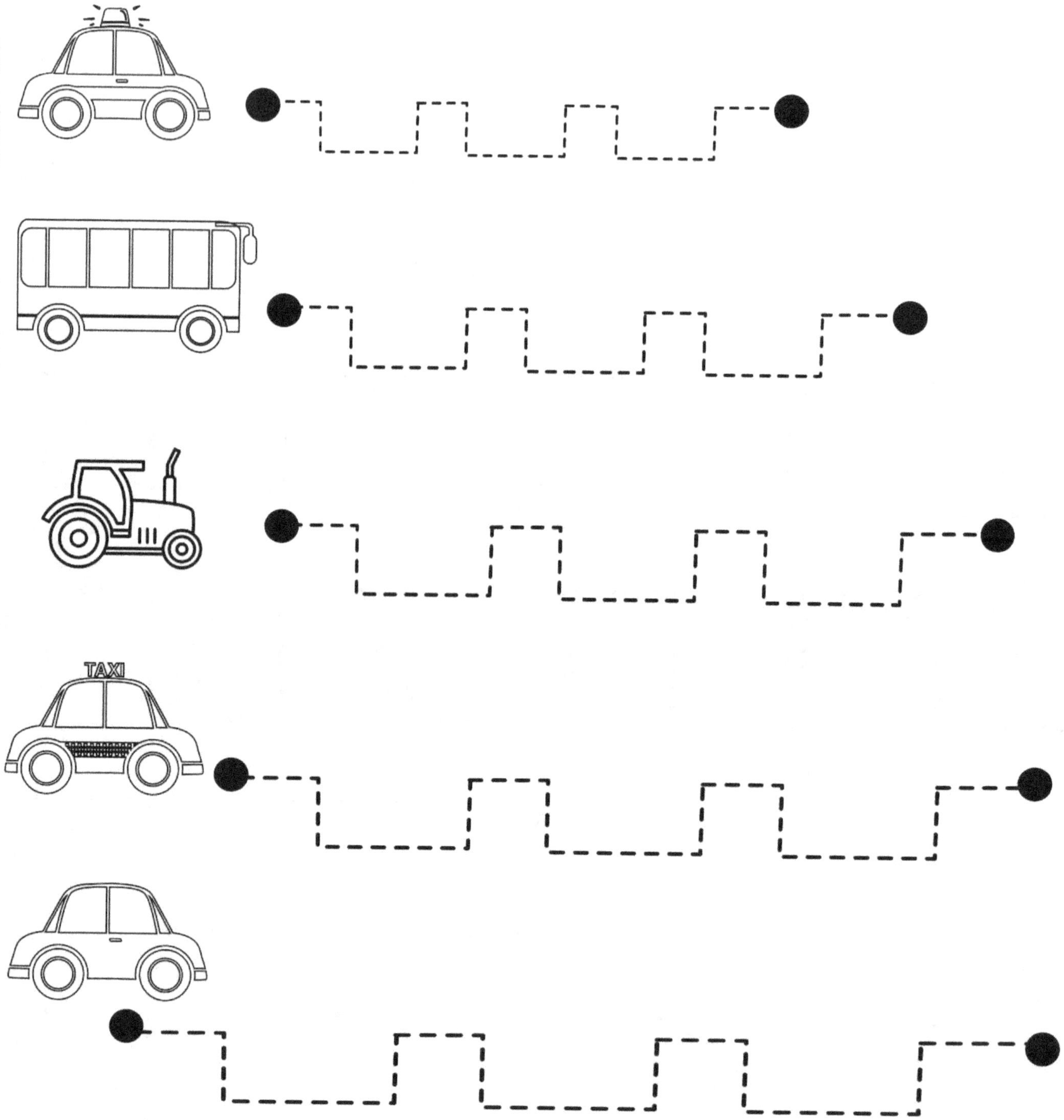

SLANTING LINES

Trace the dotted slanting lines.
Right to left.

# SLANTING LINES

Trace the dotted slanting lines.
Left to right.

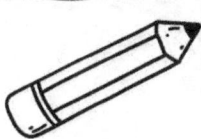 

SLANTING LINES

Trace the sun rays.

 # SLANTING LINES
Trace the rain shower.

 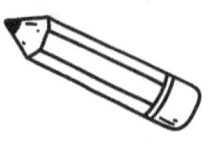

LOOP LINES

Trace the dotted loop lines.
Help the snail find his friend.

LOOP LINES

Trace the dotted loop lines.
Help the worm find the apple.

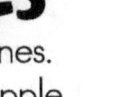

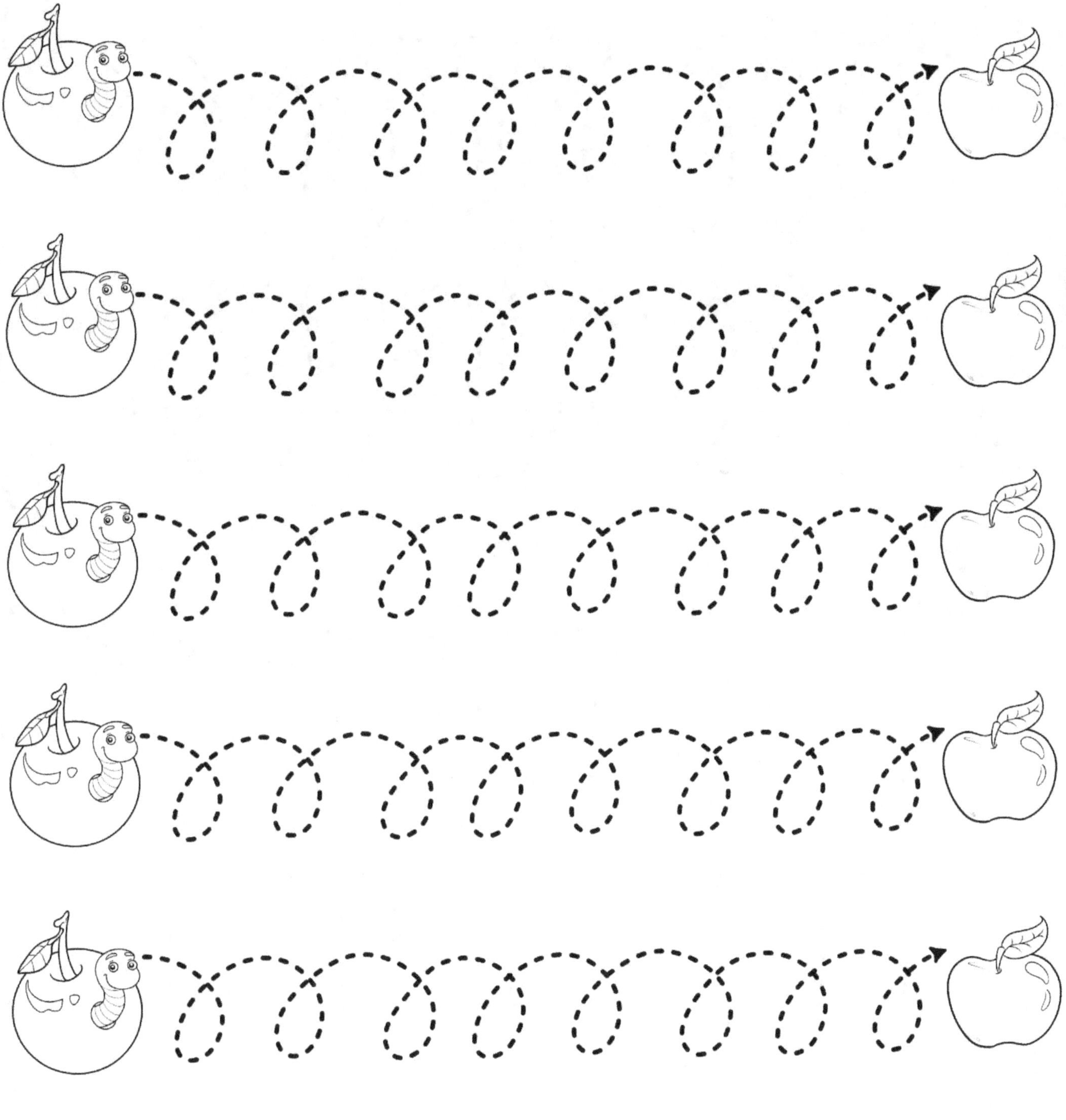

LOOP LINES

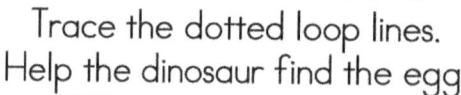

Trace the dotted loop lines.
Help the dinosaur find the egg.

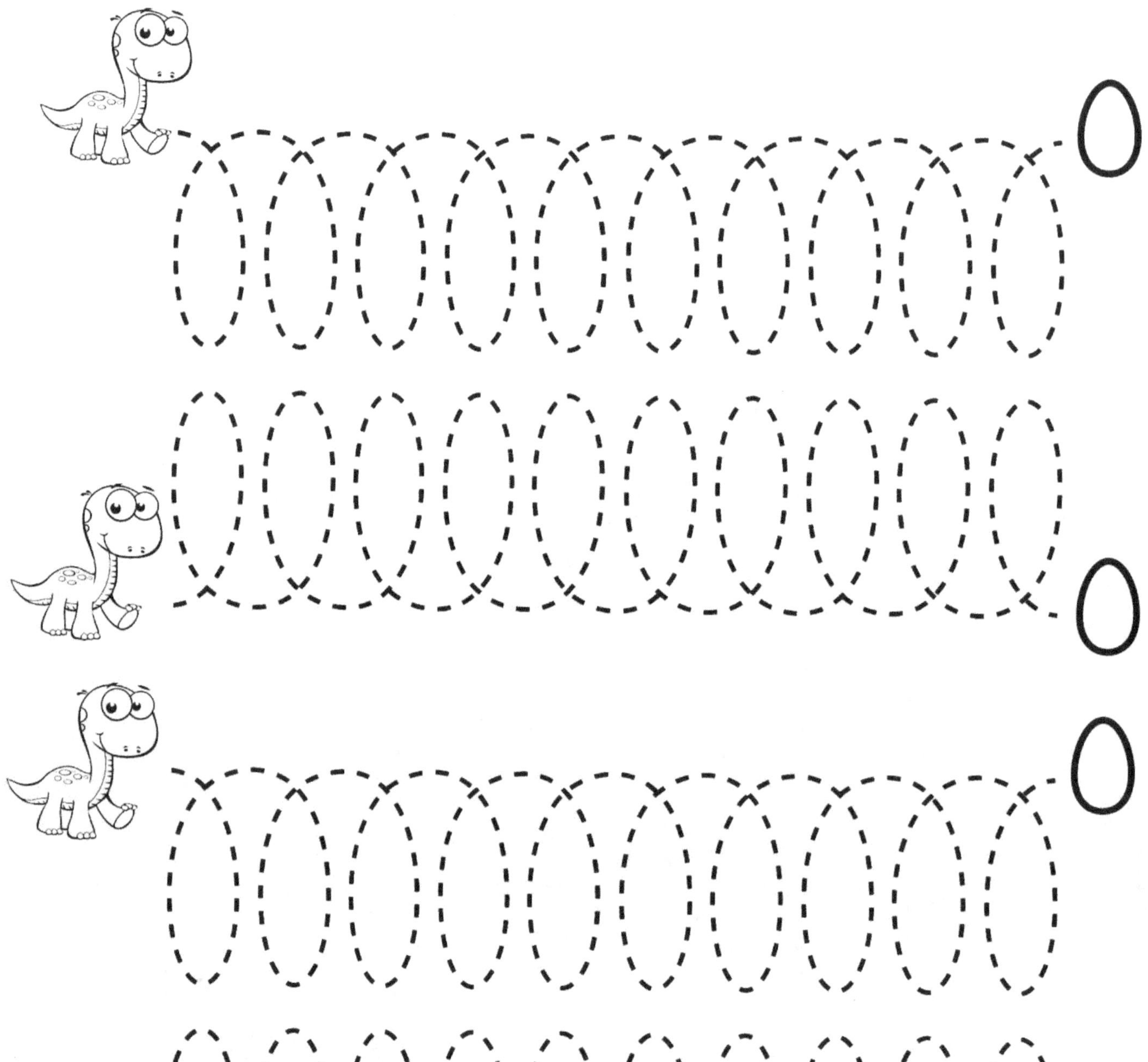

 # LOOP LINES

Trace the dotted loop lines.
Trace the planet and stars.
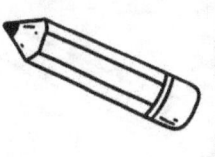

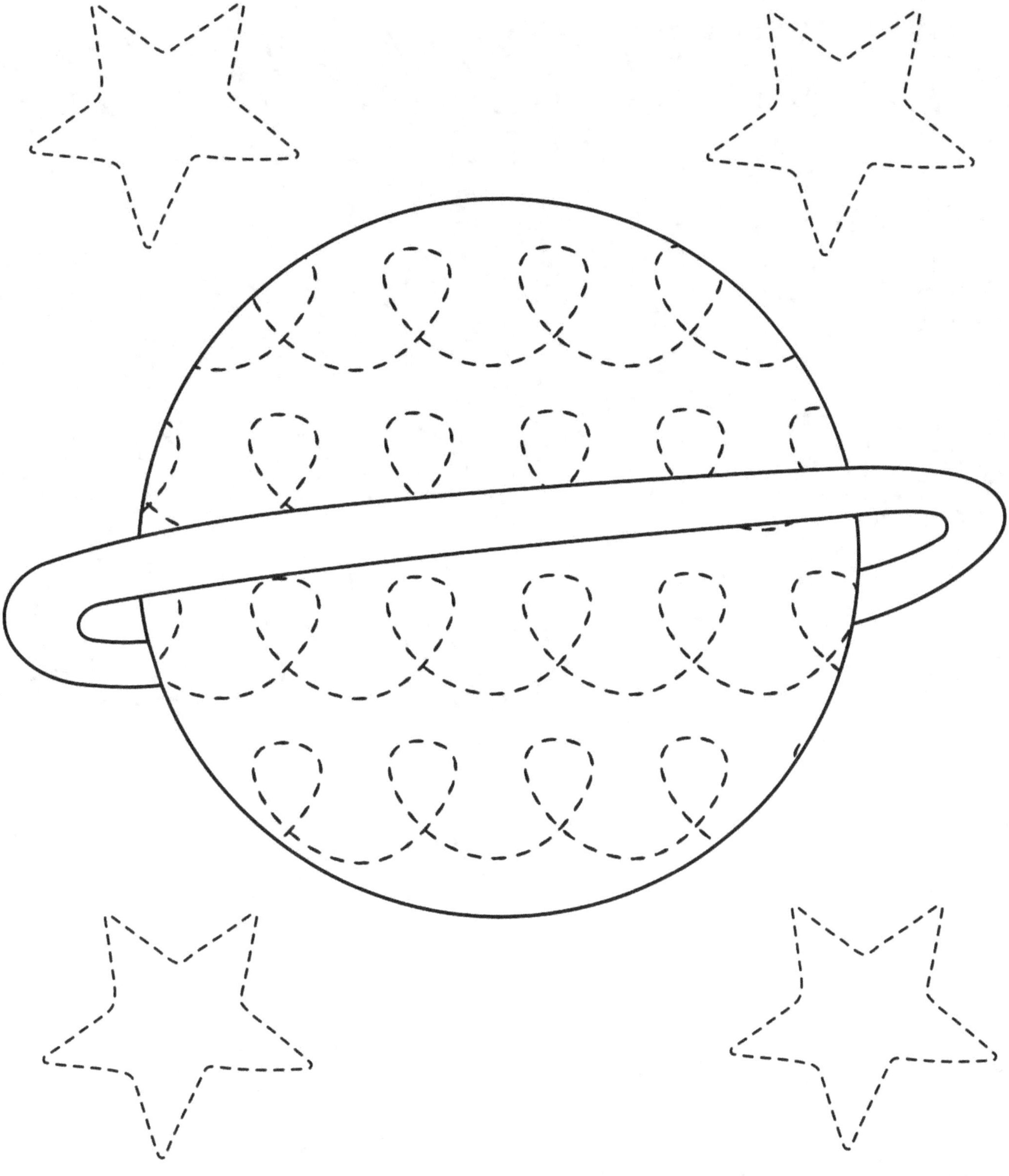

 # WAVY LINES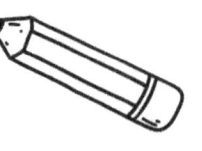

Trace the dotted wavy lines.
Help the astronaut find the spaceship.

 # WAVY LINES
Trace the dotted wavy lines.
Connect the flowers with the pot.
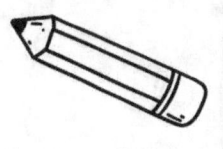

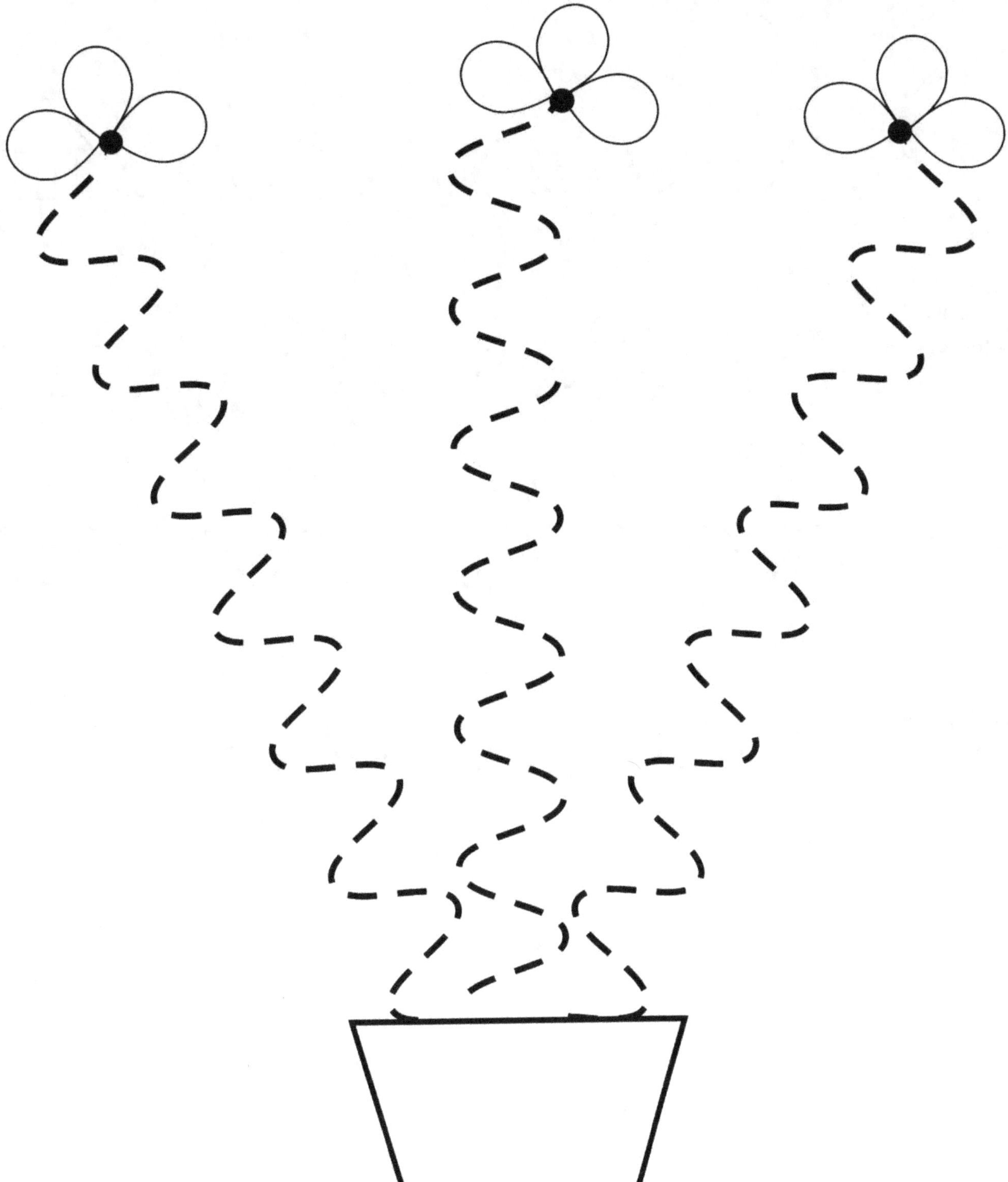

WAVY LINES

Trace the dotted wavy lines.
Help the car drive home.

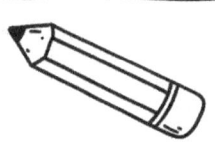

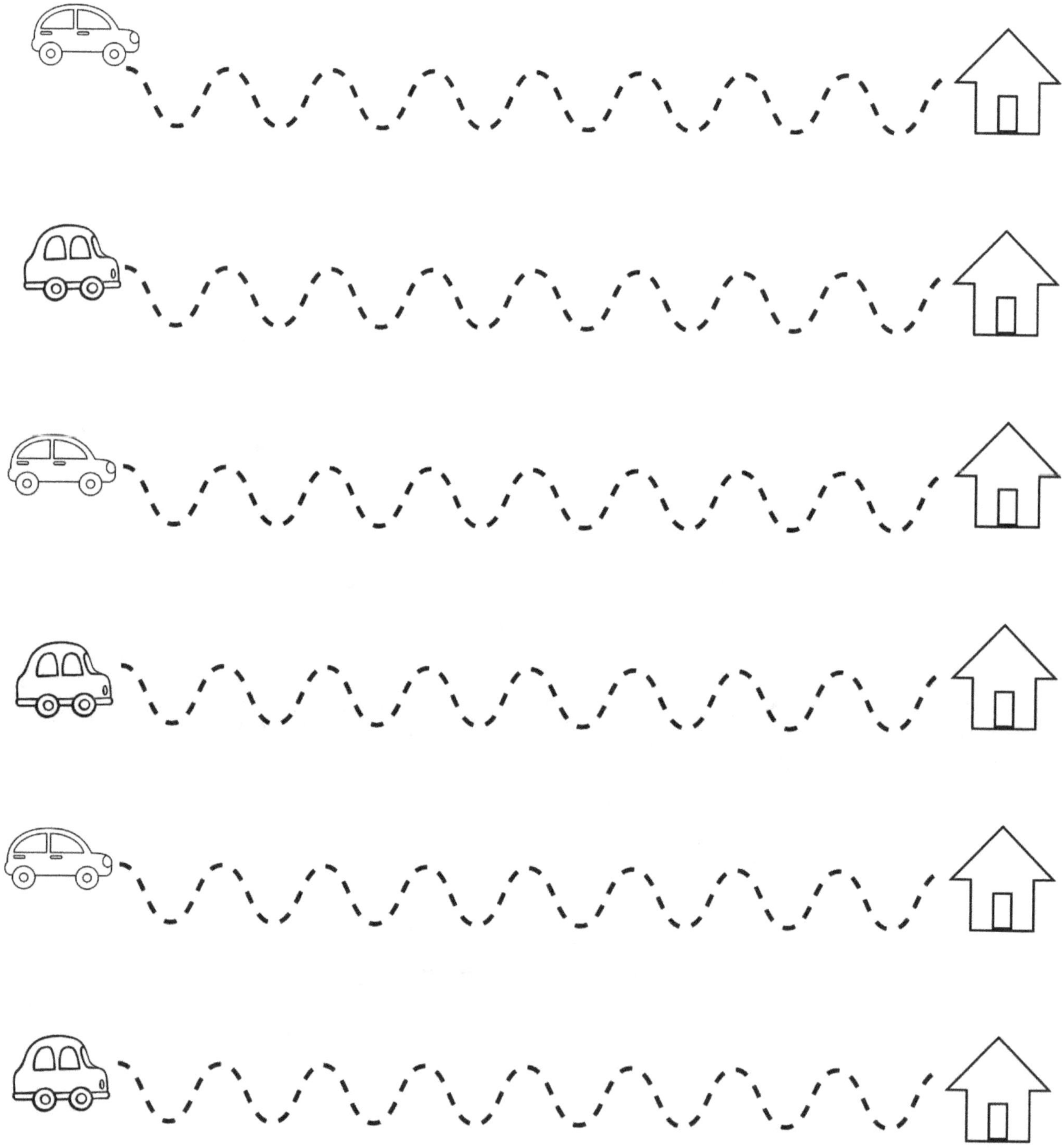

 # WAVY LINES

Trace the dotted wavy lines.
Help the rabbit find the carrot.

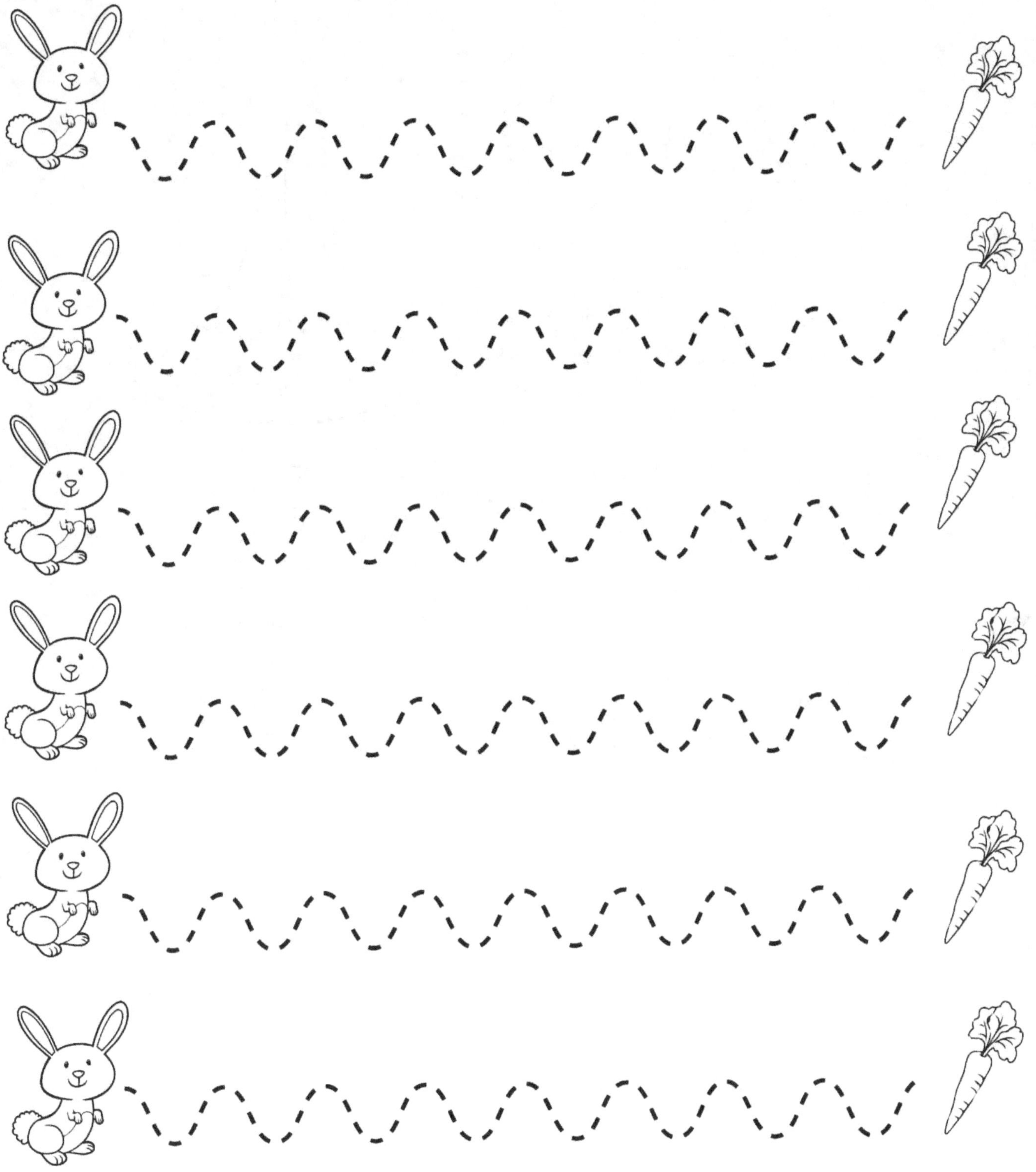

 # WAVY LINES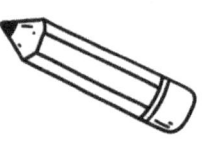
Trace the dotted wavy lines.
Trace the boat and the sea waves.

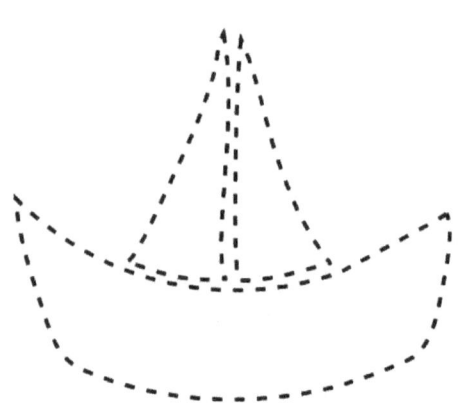

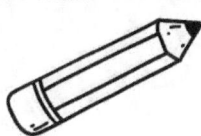 # WAVY LINES
Trace the dotted wavy balloon strings.

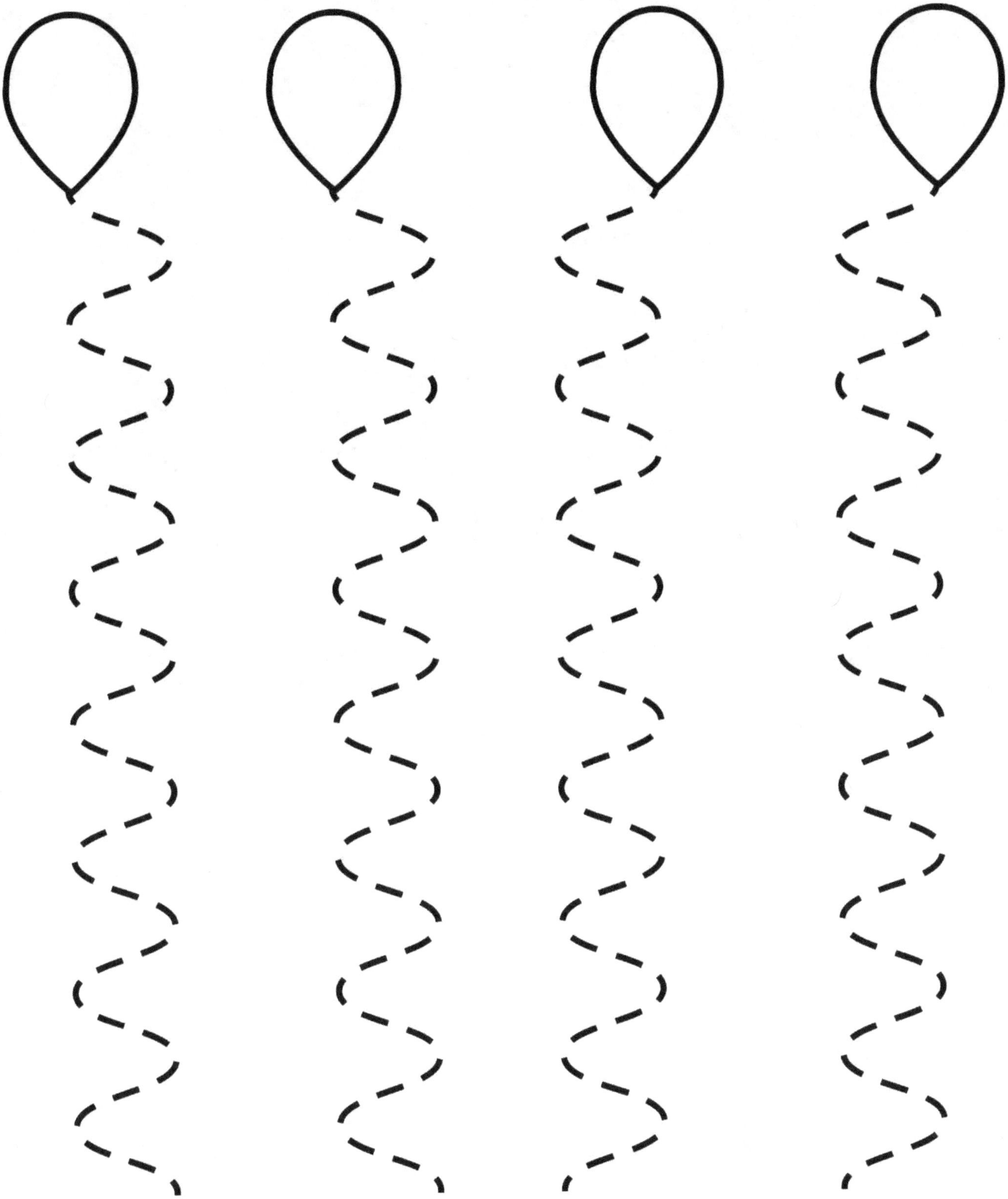

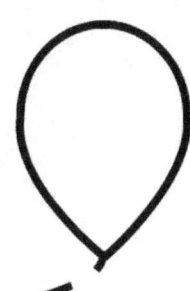

 # CURVED LINES

Trace the hat and dotted curved lines.

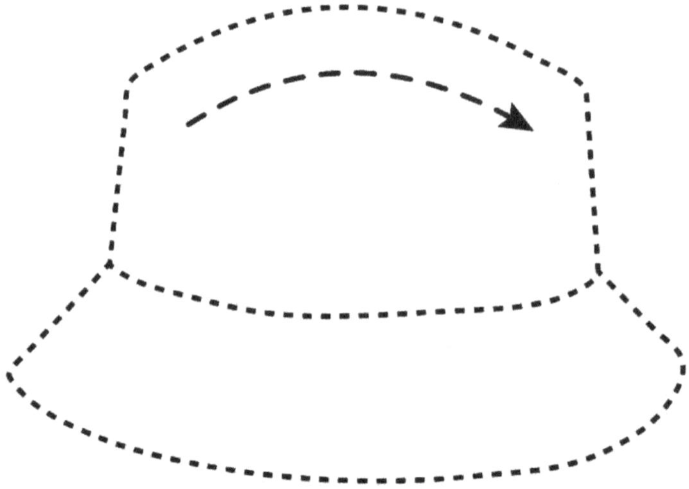

# CURVED LINES

Trace the dotted curved lines.
Help the boat find the island.

 # CURVED LINES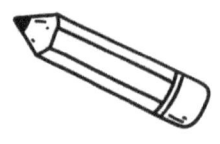
Trace the dotted curved lines.
Help the fish find her babies.

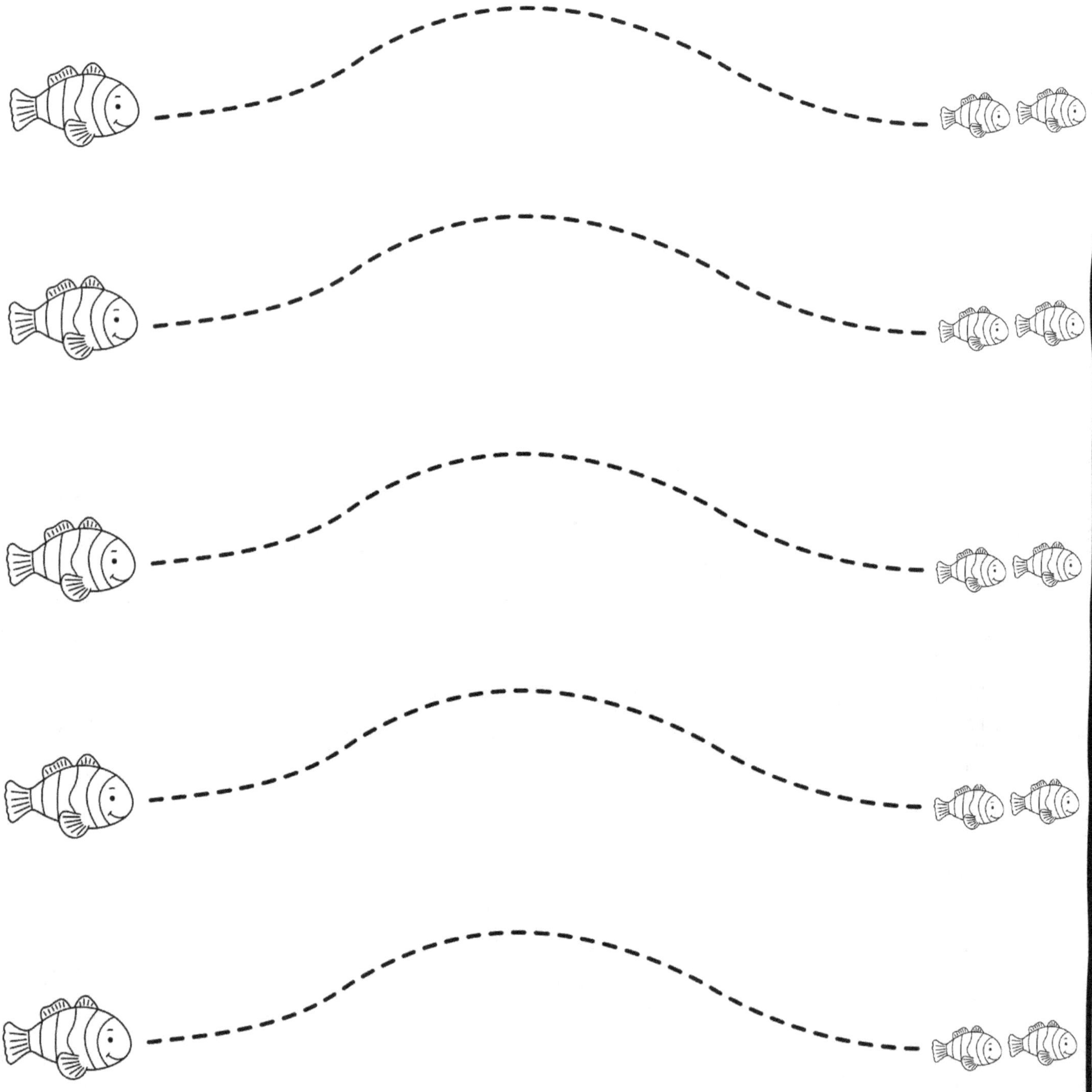

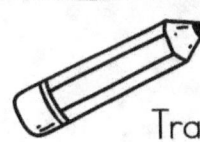 # CURVED LINES

Trace the dotted curved lines and color the pear.

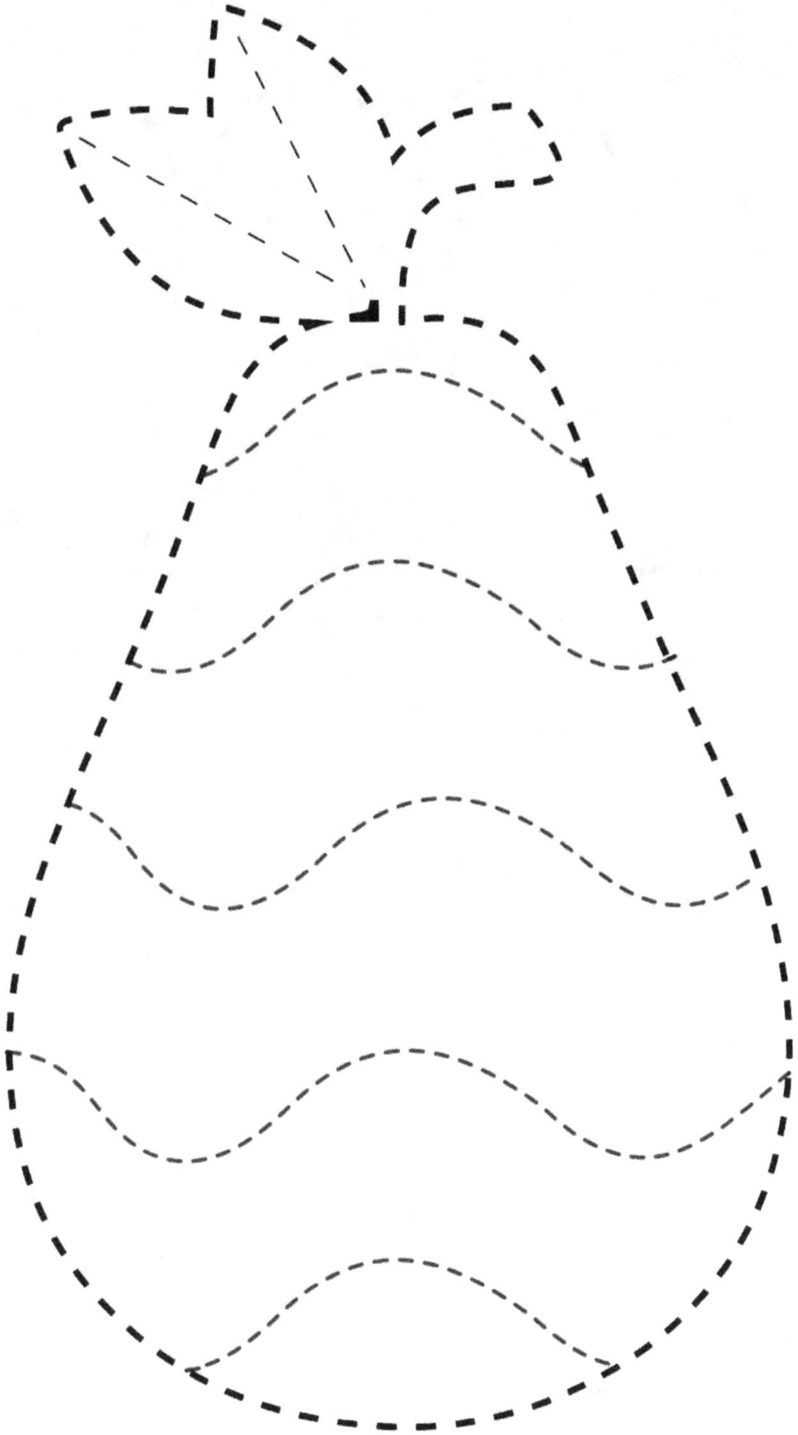

 # CURVED LINES

Trace the dotted curved lines and color the butterflies.

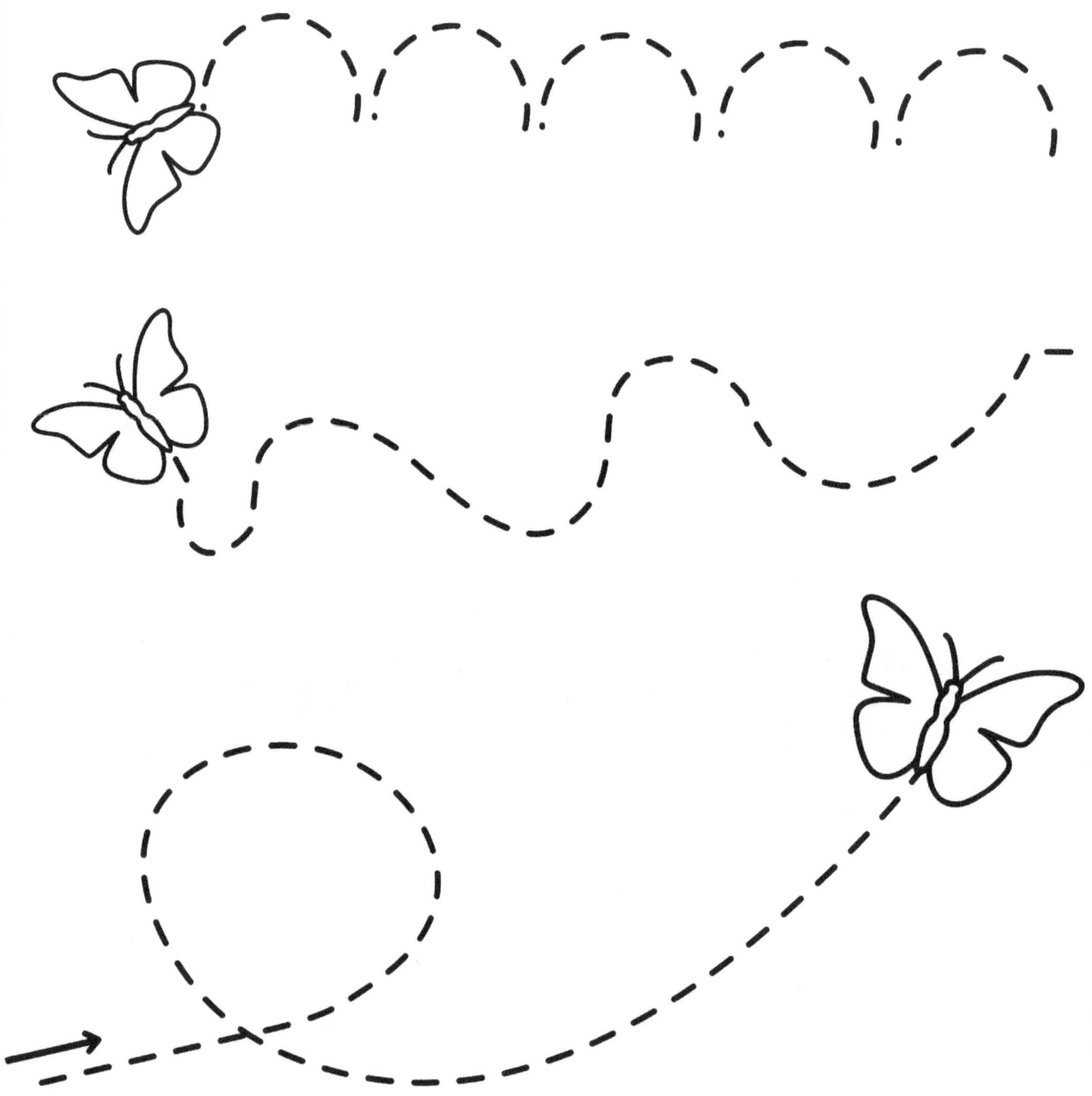

 # SPIRAL LINES

Trace the dotted curved lines.
Help the snail on it's travels.

 # TRACE THE DOTTED LINES

Connect the flowers with the pots.

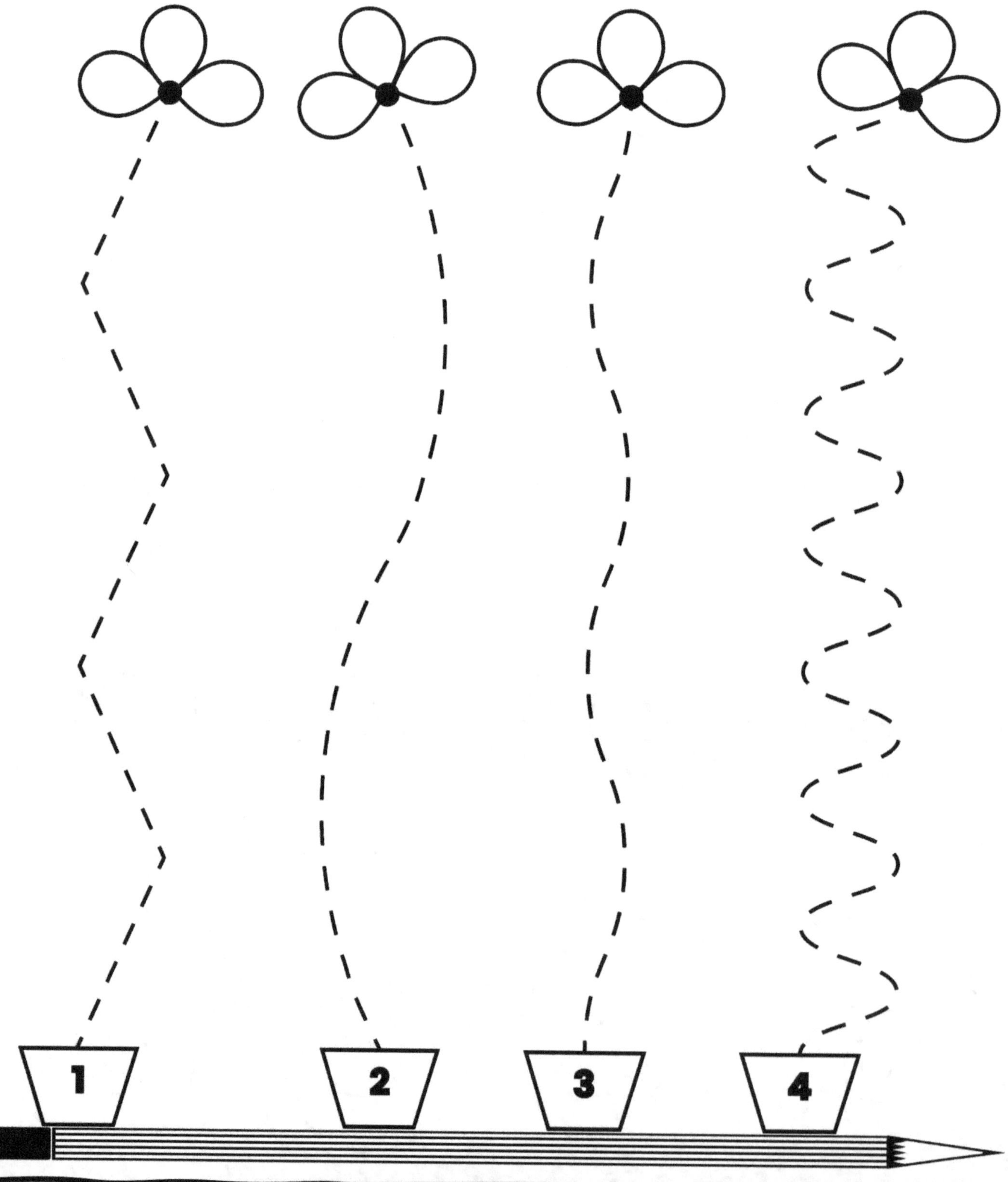

1

2

3

4

 # TRACE LINES

Trace the dotted lines.
Connect the rocket with outer space.

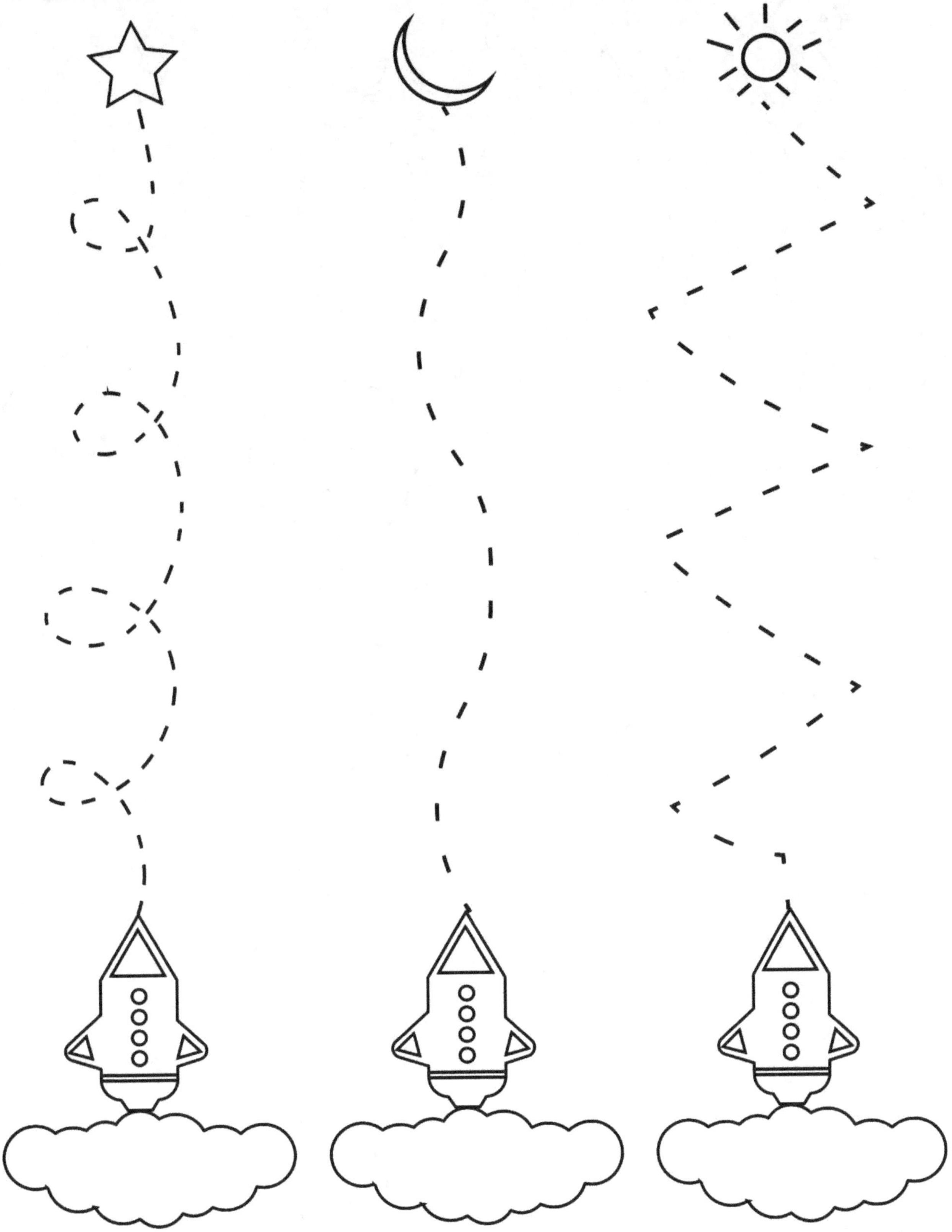

TRACE LINES

Trace the dotted lines.
Help the snake, snail and worm find the apples.

 # TRACE THE DOTTED LINE

Help the bee find it's home.

TRACE THE DOTTED LINE

Help the bus find the school.

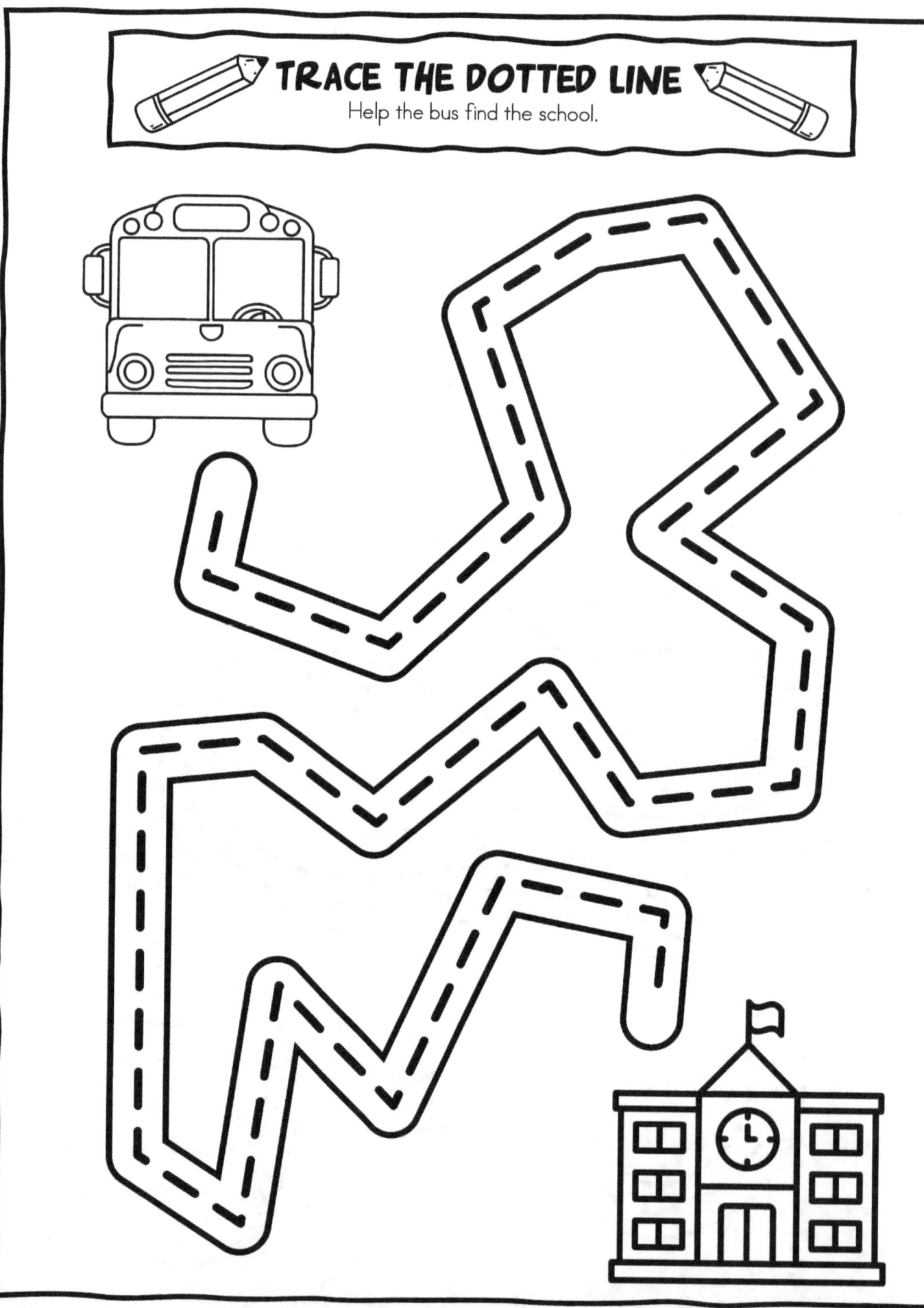

TRACE THE SHAPE

RECTANGLE

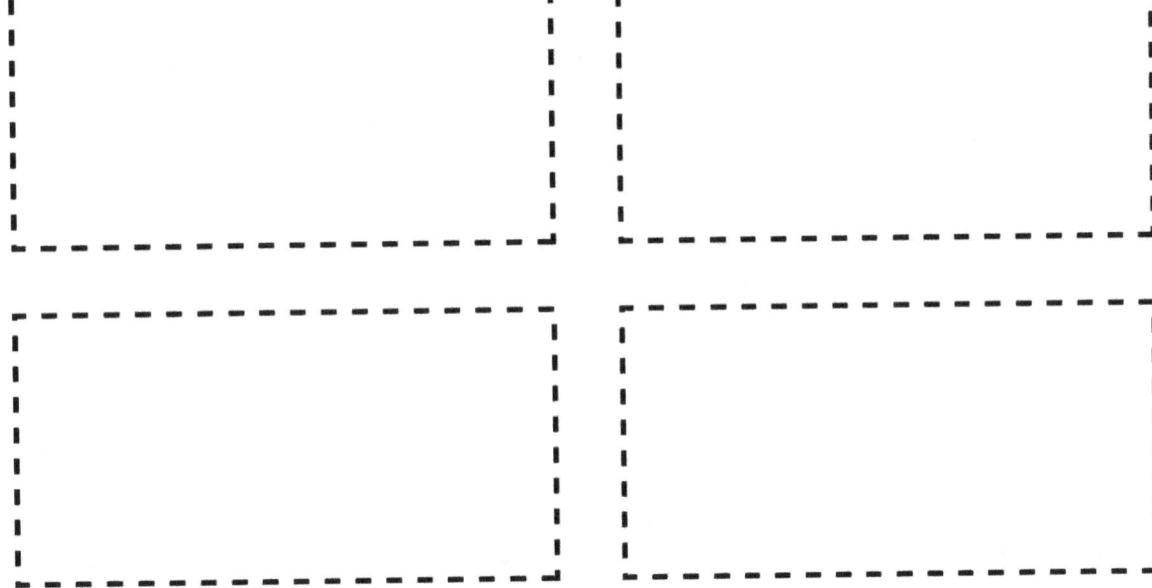

 # TRACE THE SHAPE

SQUARE

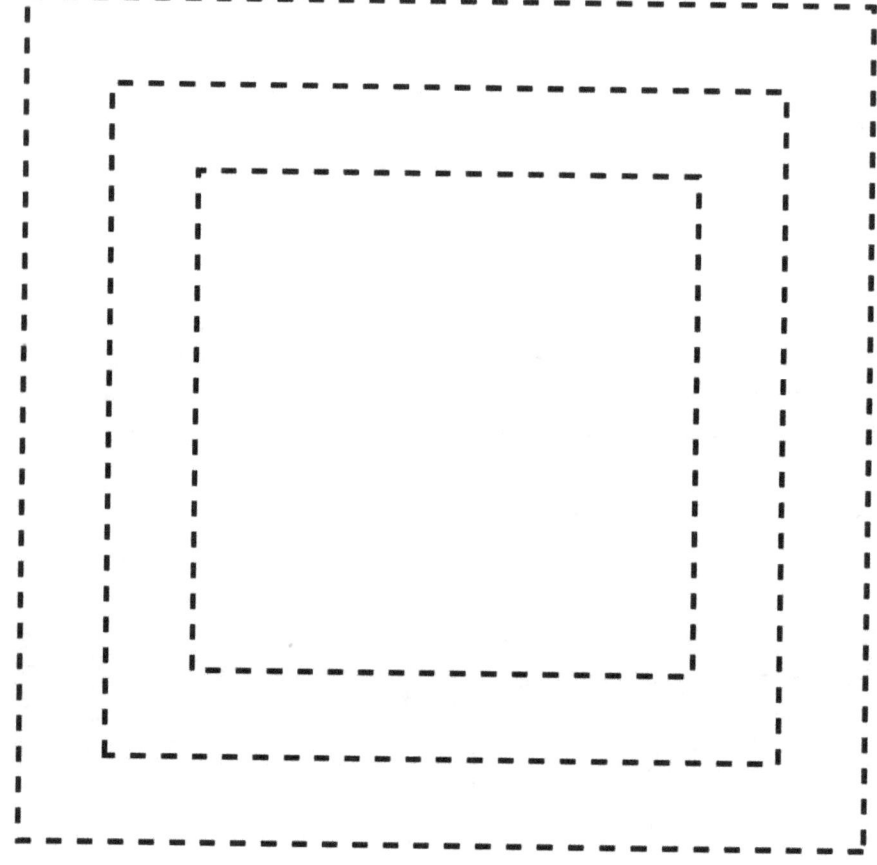

 # TRACE THE SHAPE

CIRCLE

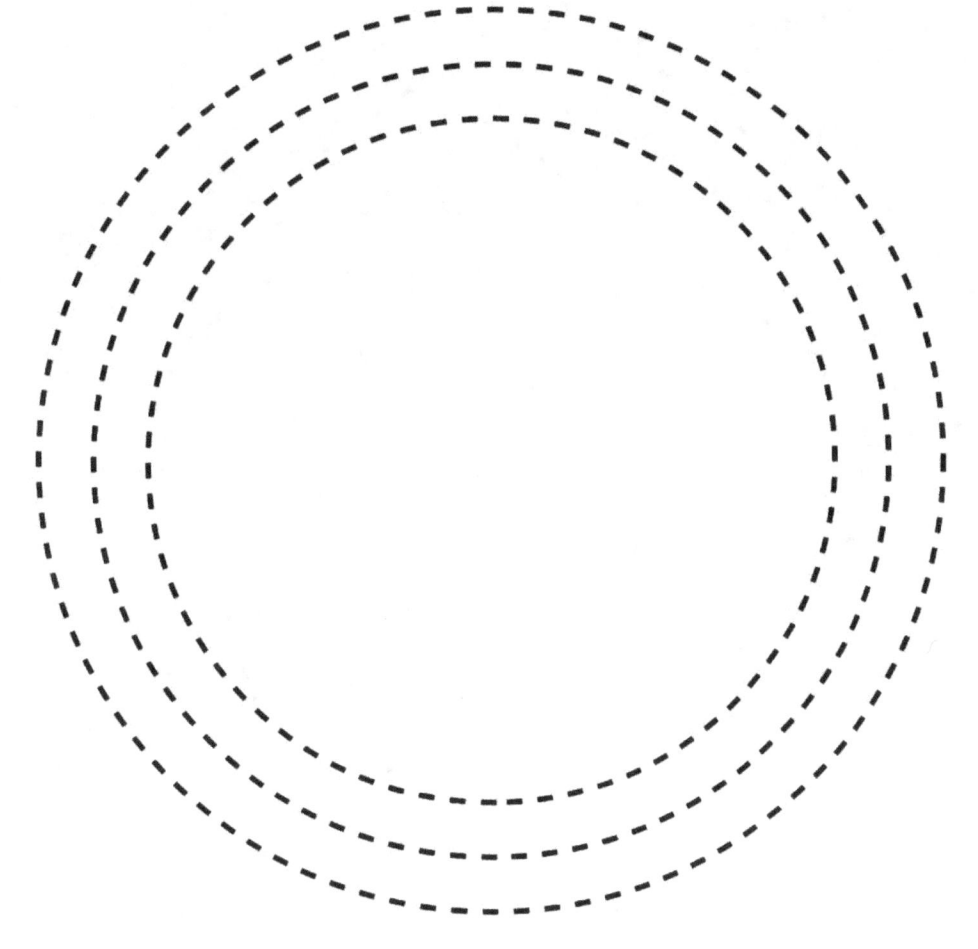

 # TRACE THE SHAPE

PENTAGON

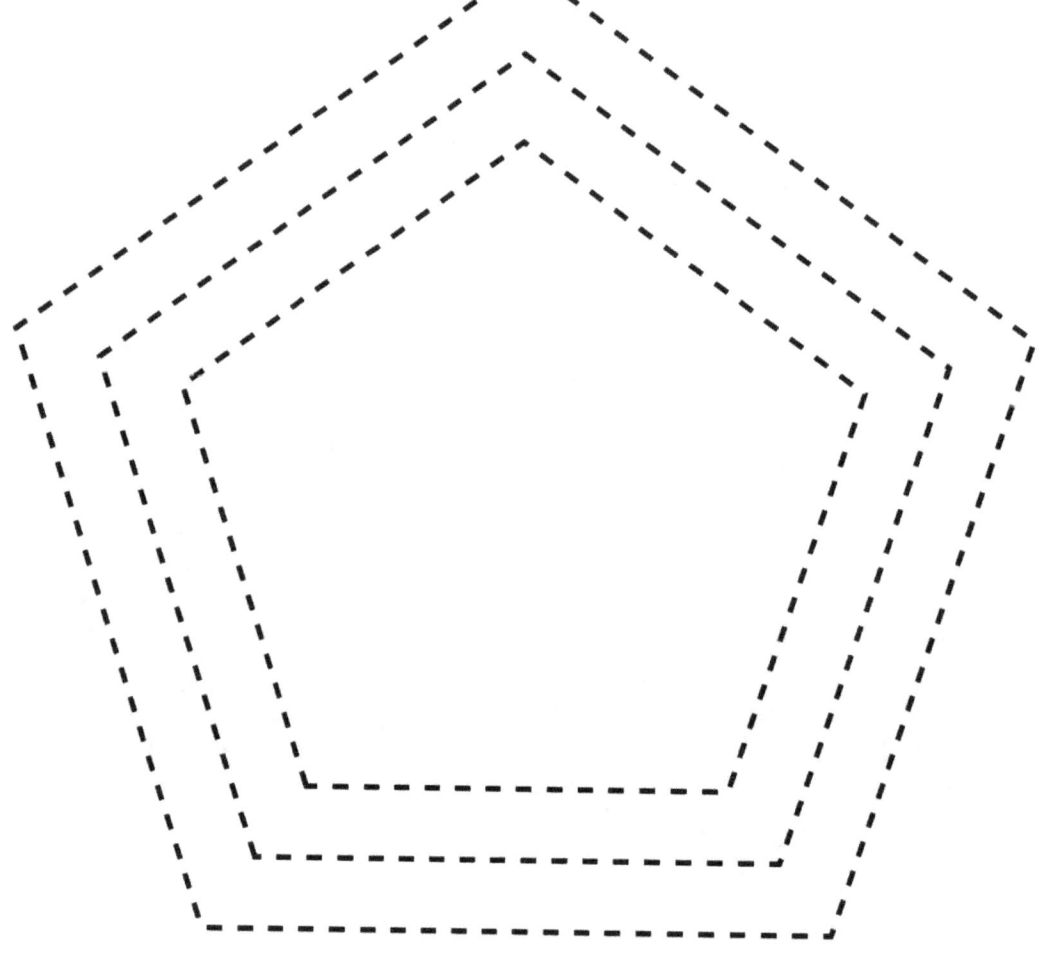

 # TRACE THE SHAPE

HEXAGON

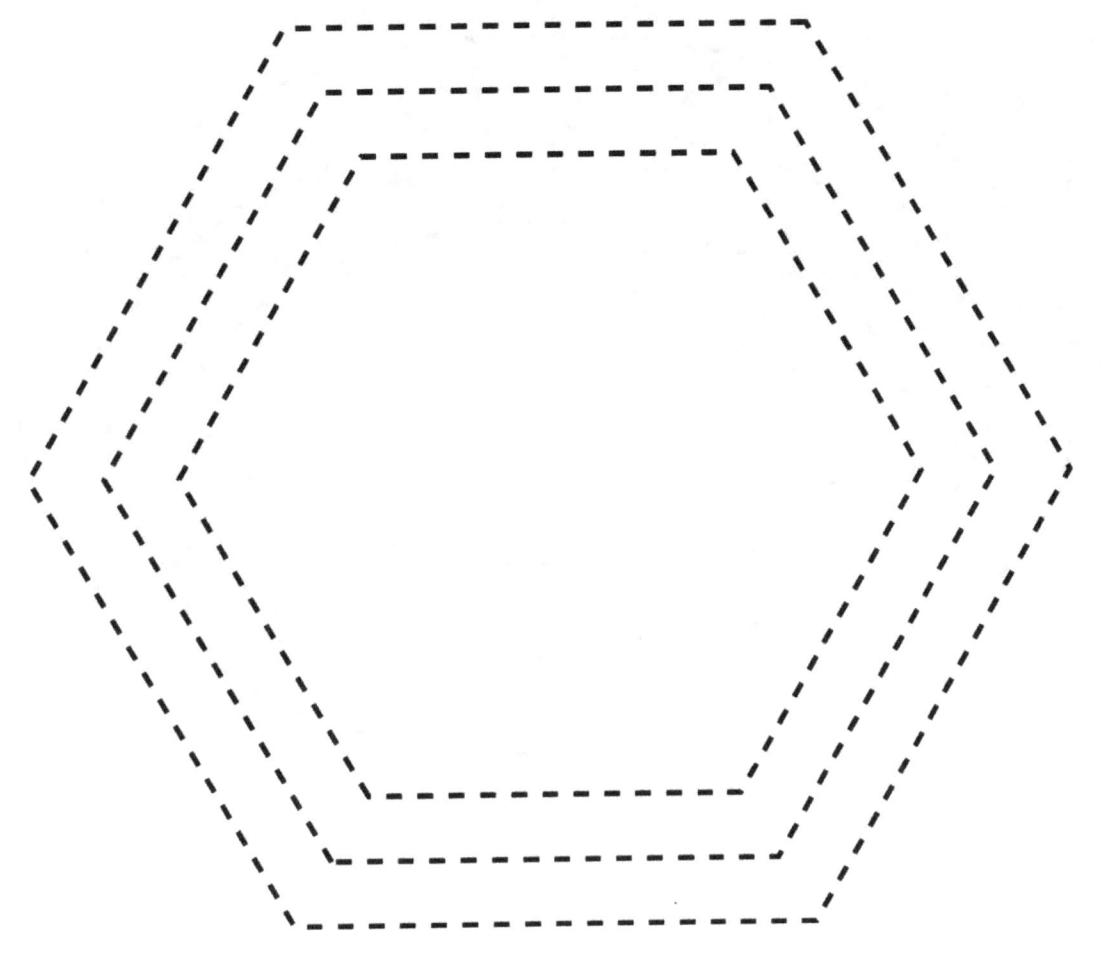

 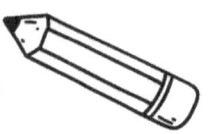

TRACE THE SHAPE

OVAL

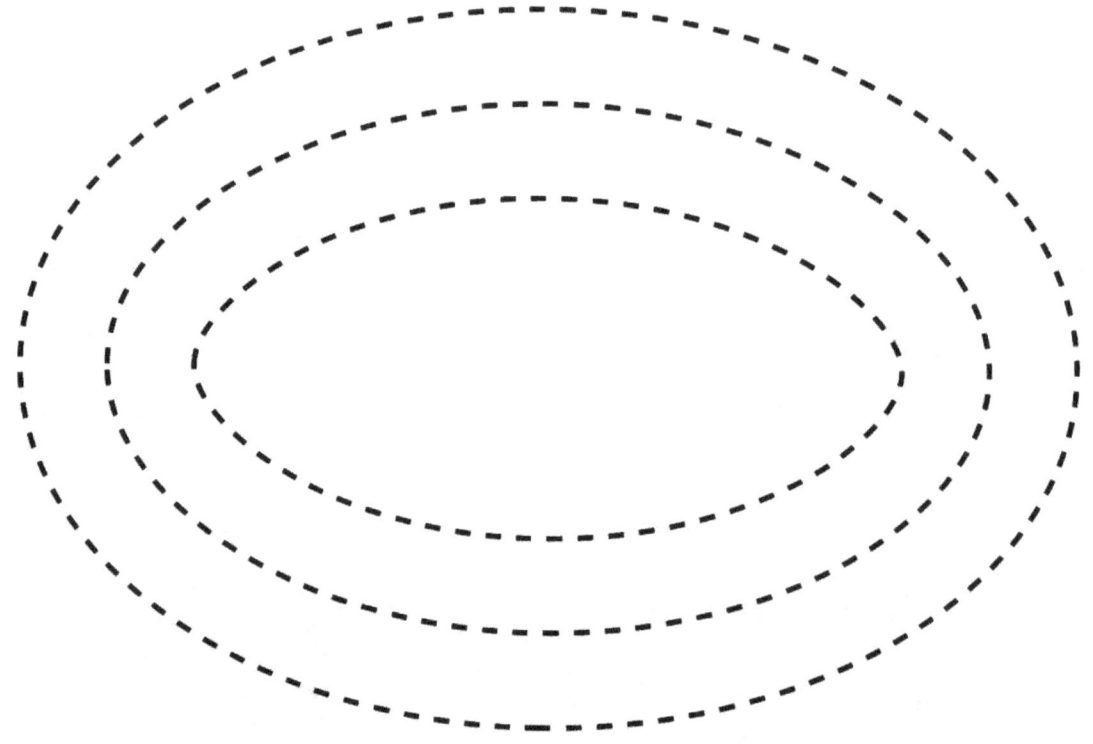

 # TRACE THE SHAPE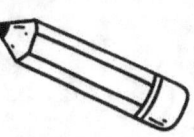

DIAMOND

TRACE THE SHAPE

TRIANGLE

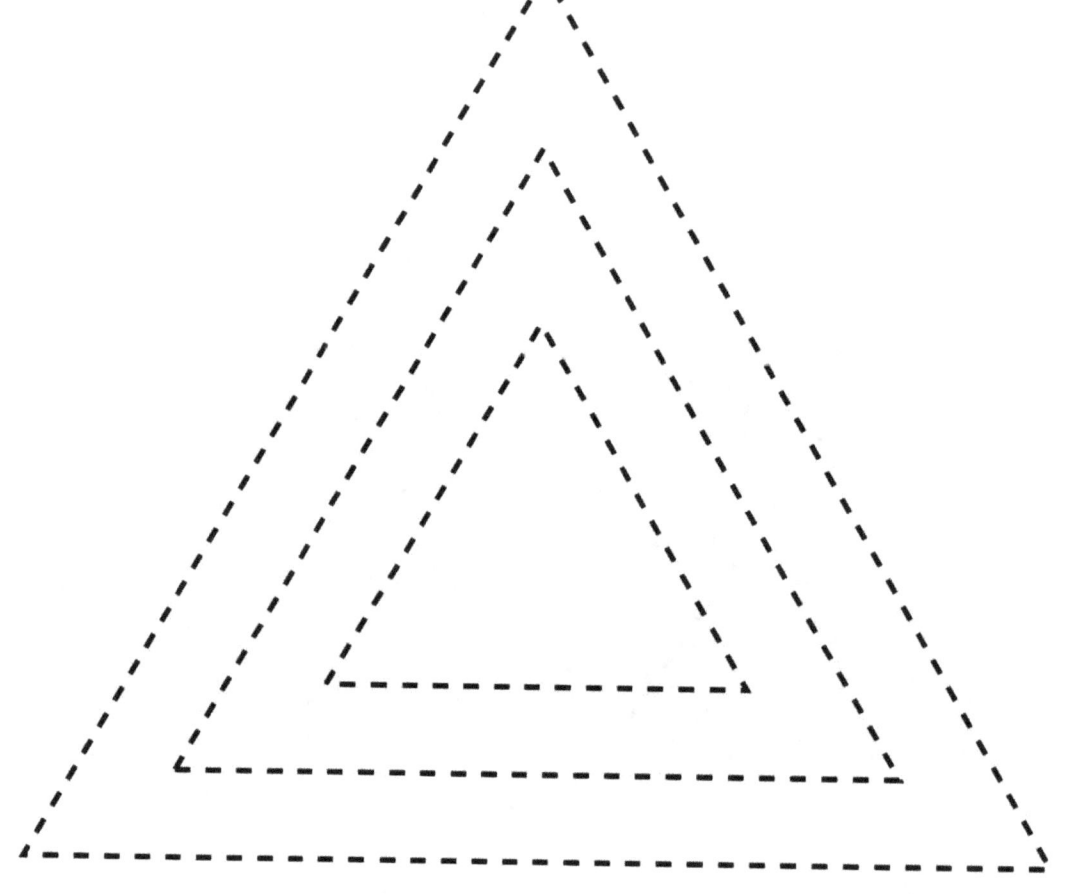

TRACE THE SHAPE

SEMICIRCLE

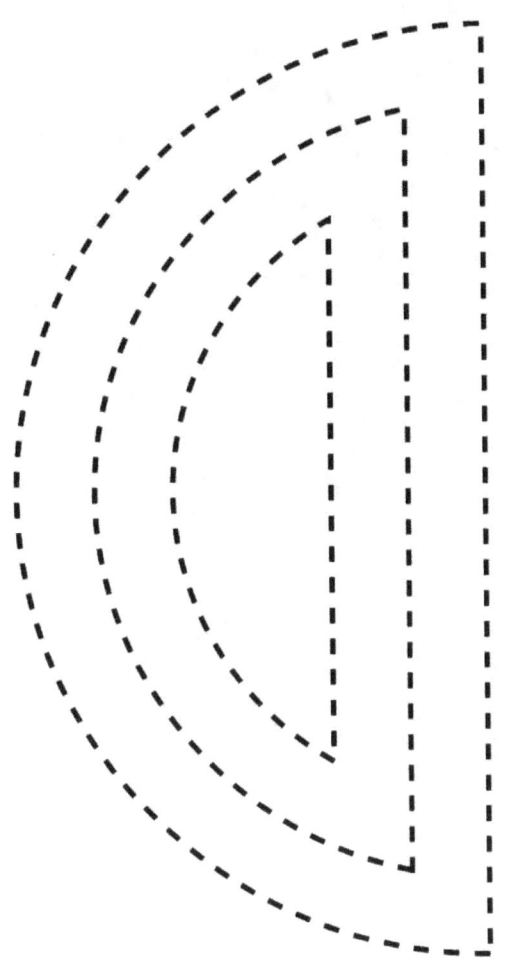

 # TRACE THE SHAPE

CRESCENT

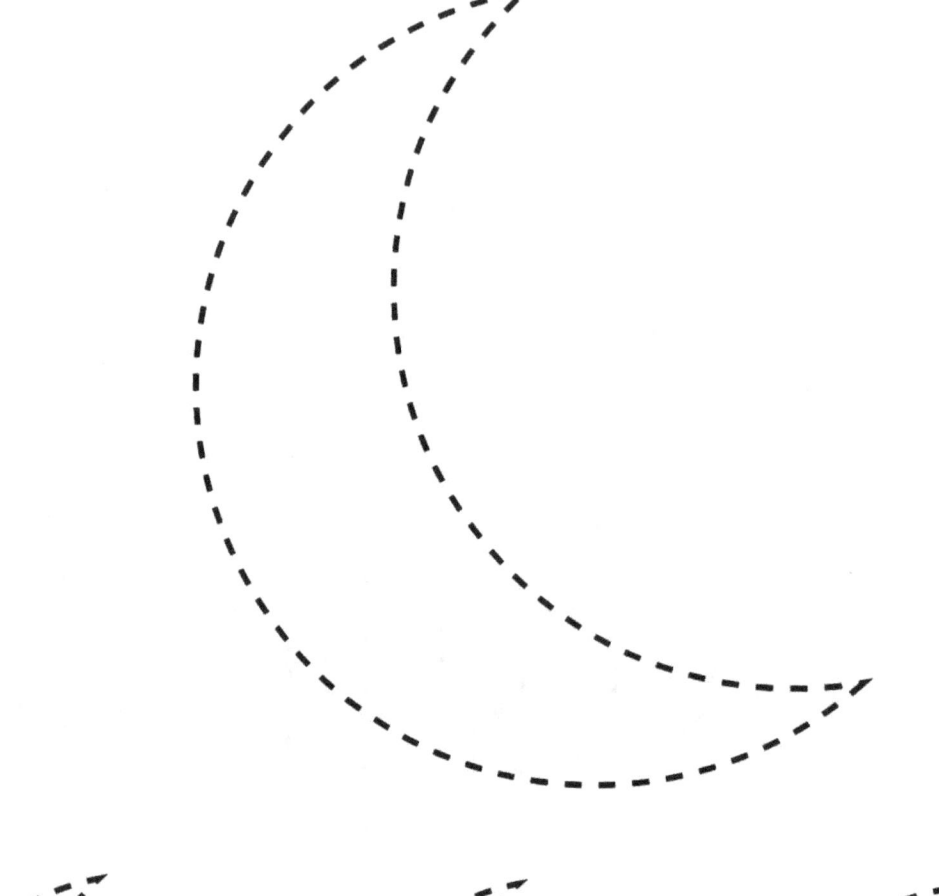

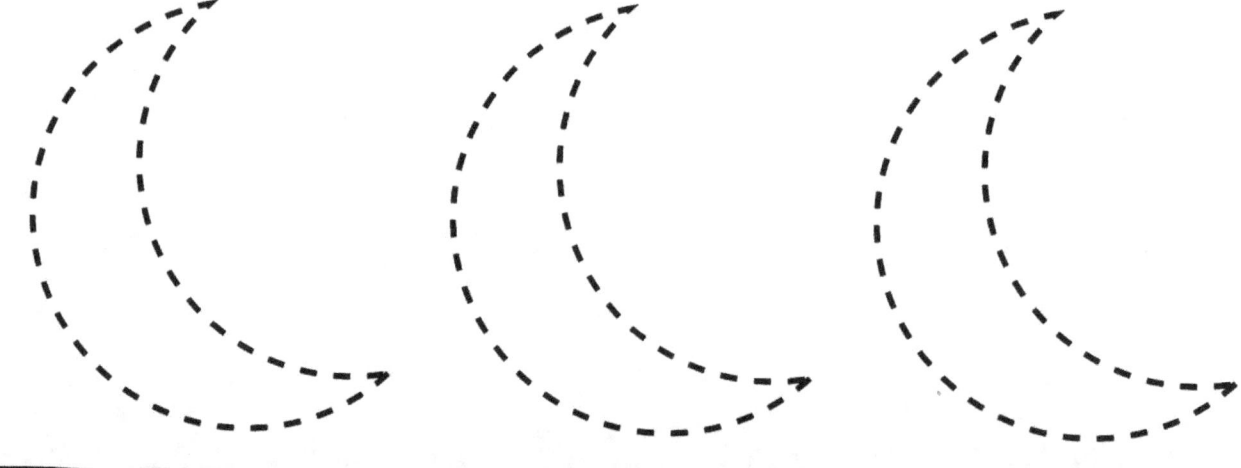

 # TRACE THE SHAPE

STAR

 # TRACE THE SHAPE

HEART

 # TRACE THE SHAPE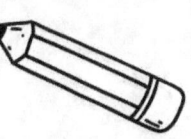

ARROW

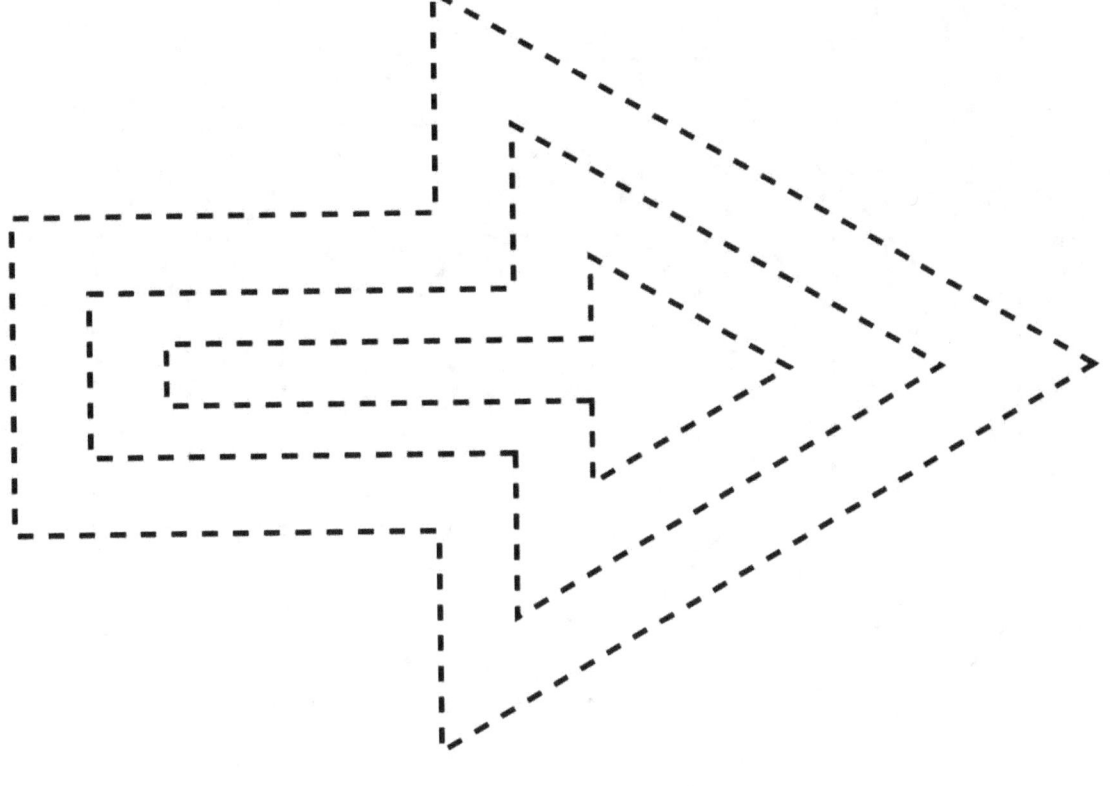

 # TRACE THE SHAPE

OCTAGON

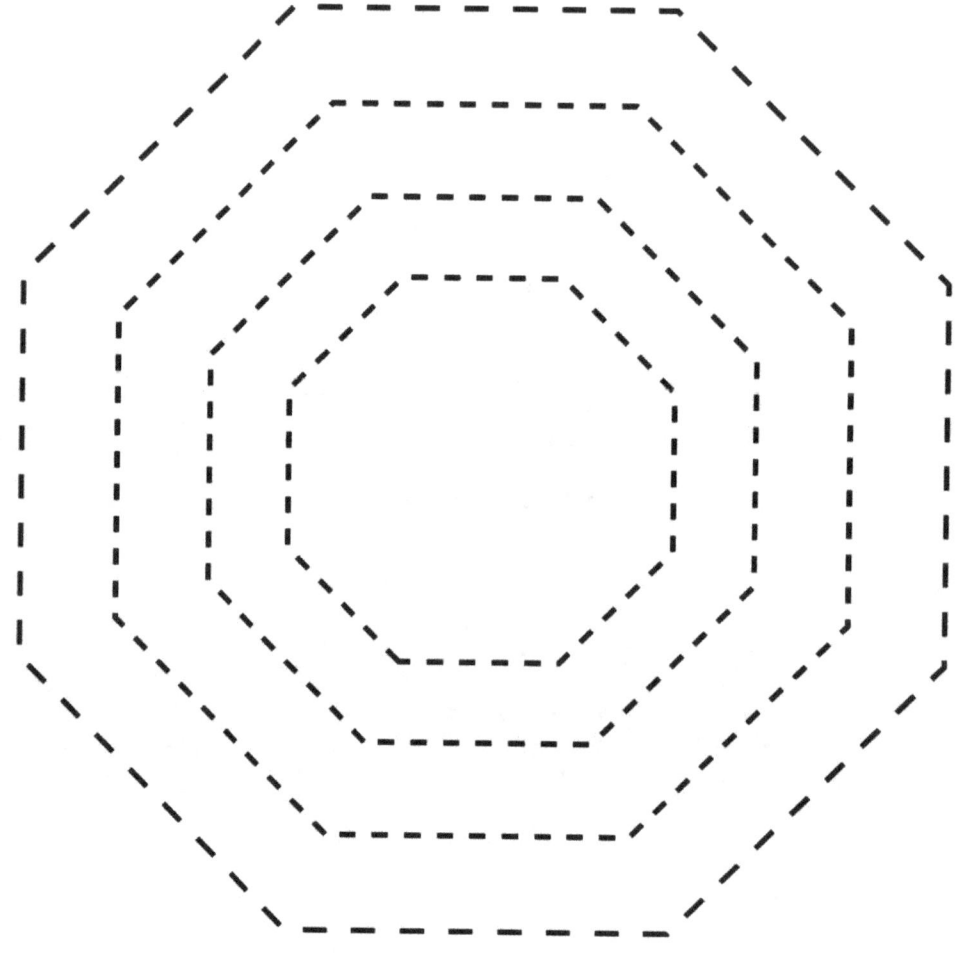

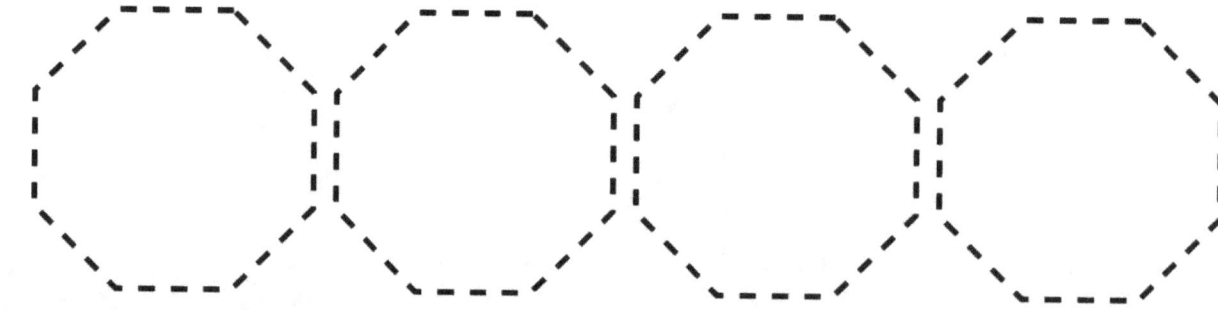

 # TRACE THE SHAPE

KITE

 # TRACE AND COLOR

 # TRACE AND COLOR

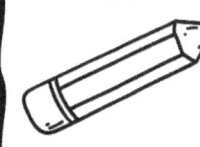 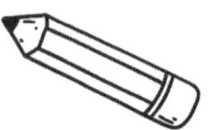 # TRACE AND COLOR

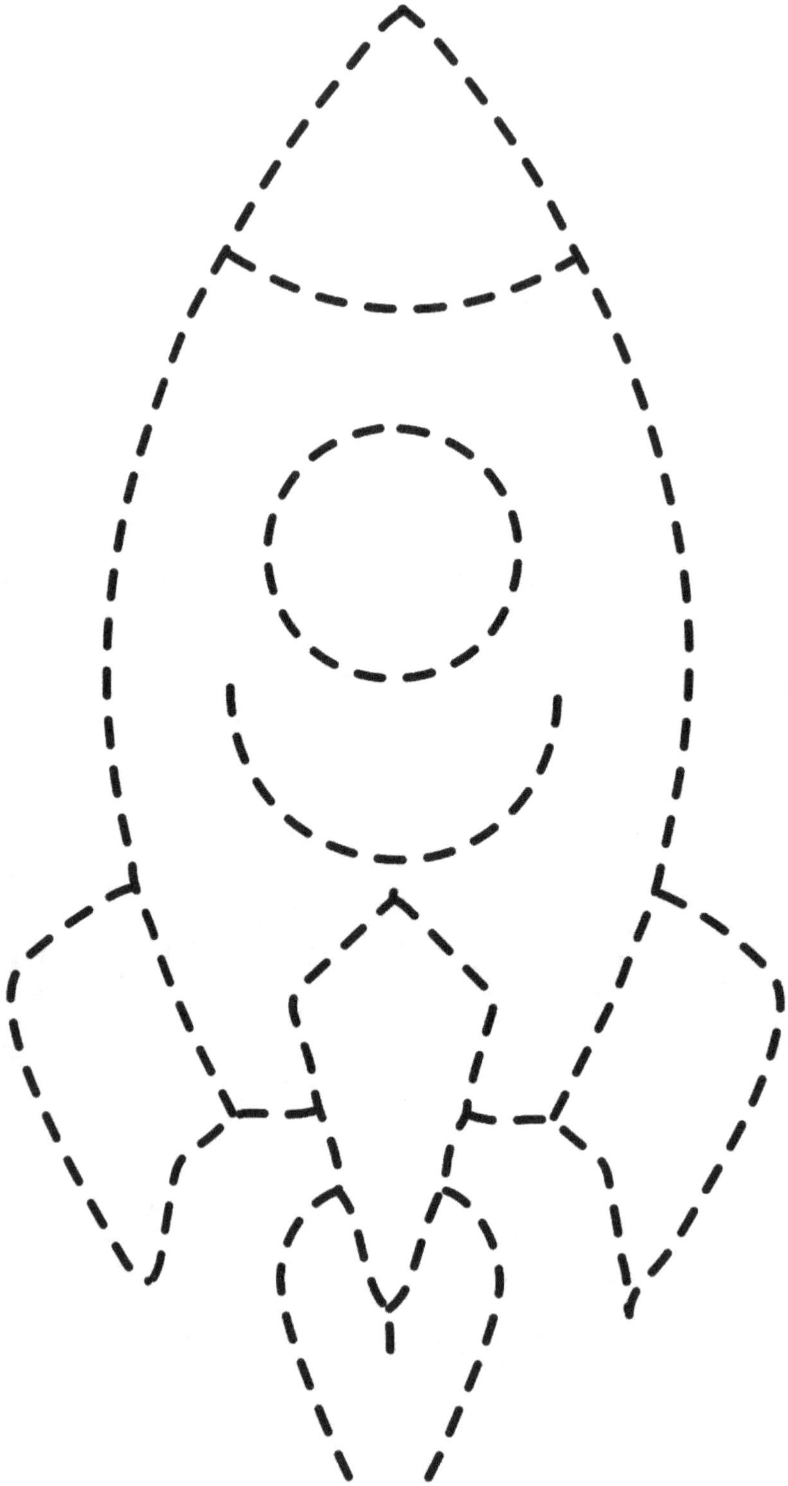

 # TRACE AND COLOR

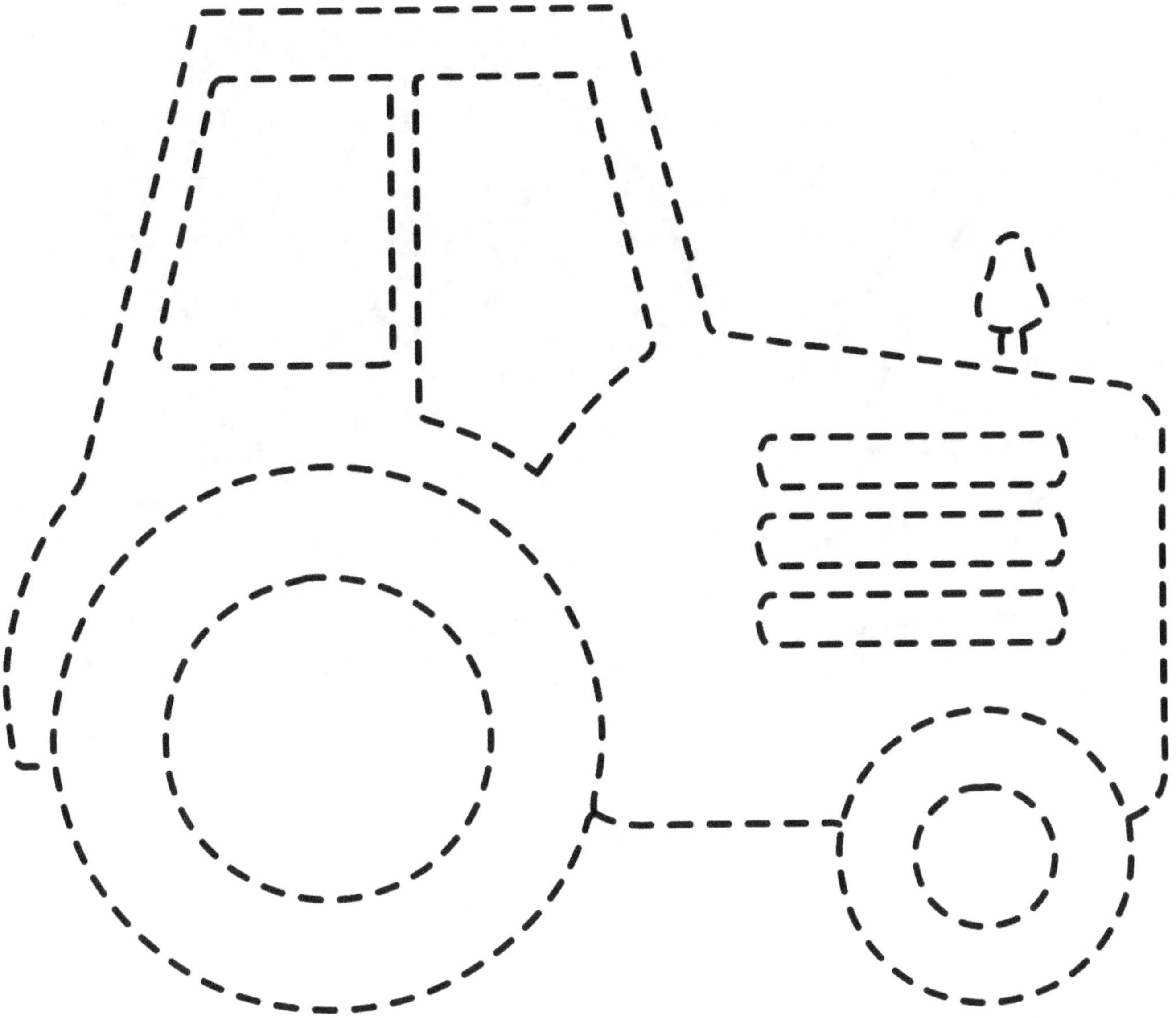

 # TRACE AND COLOR

 # TRACE AND COLOR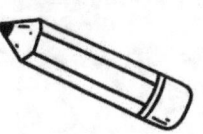

 # TRACE AND COLOR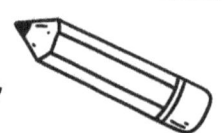

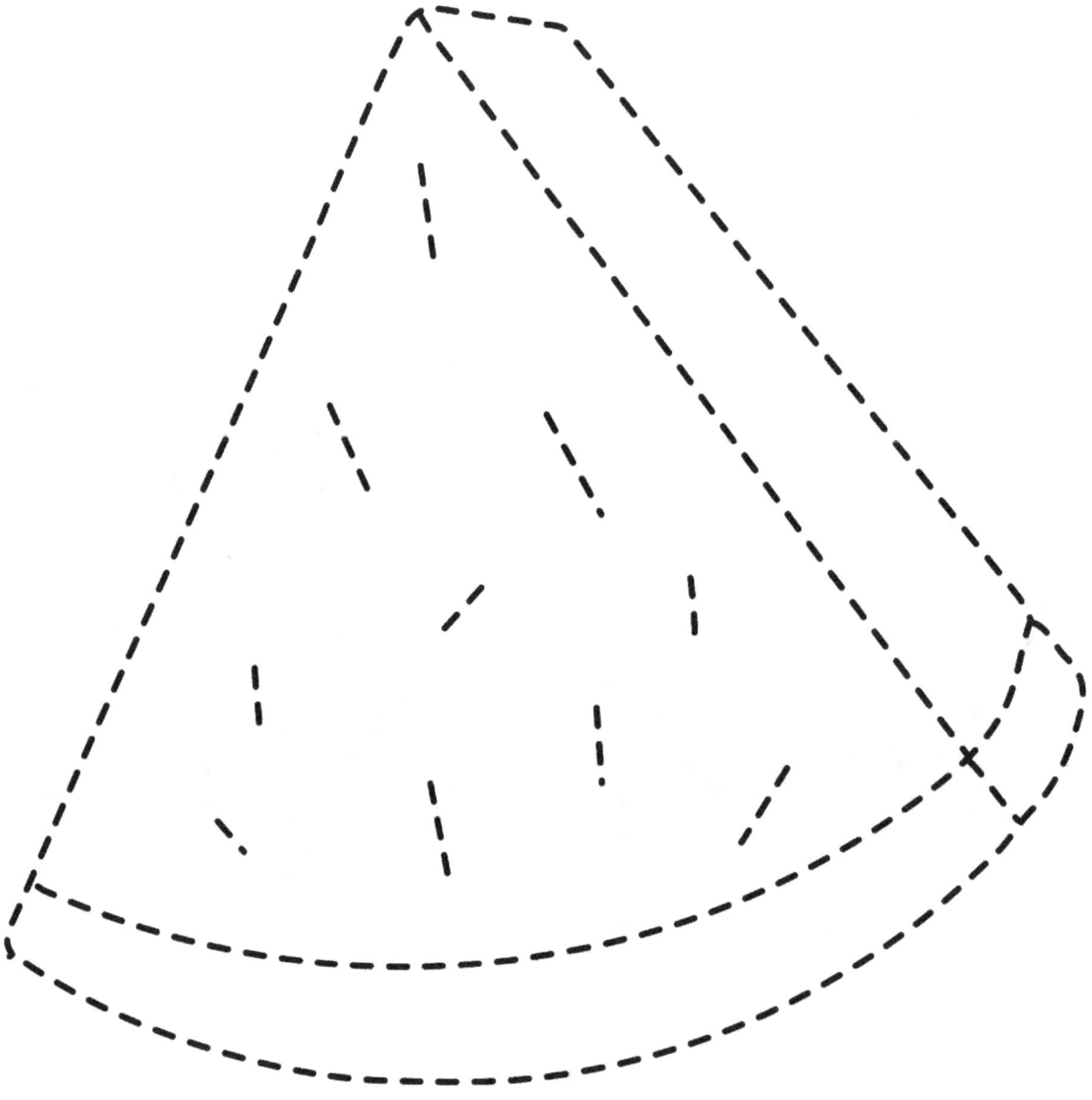

 # TRACE AND COLOR

 # TRACE AND COLOR

 # TRACE AND COLOR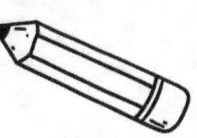

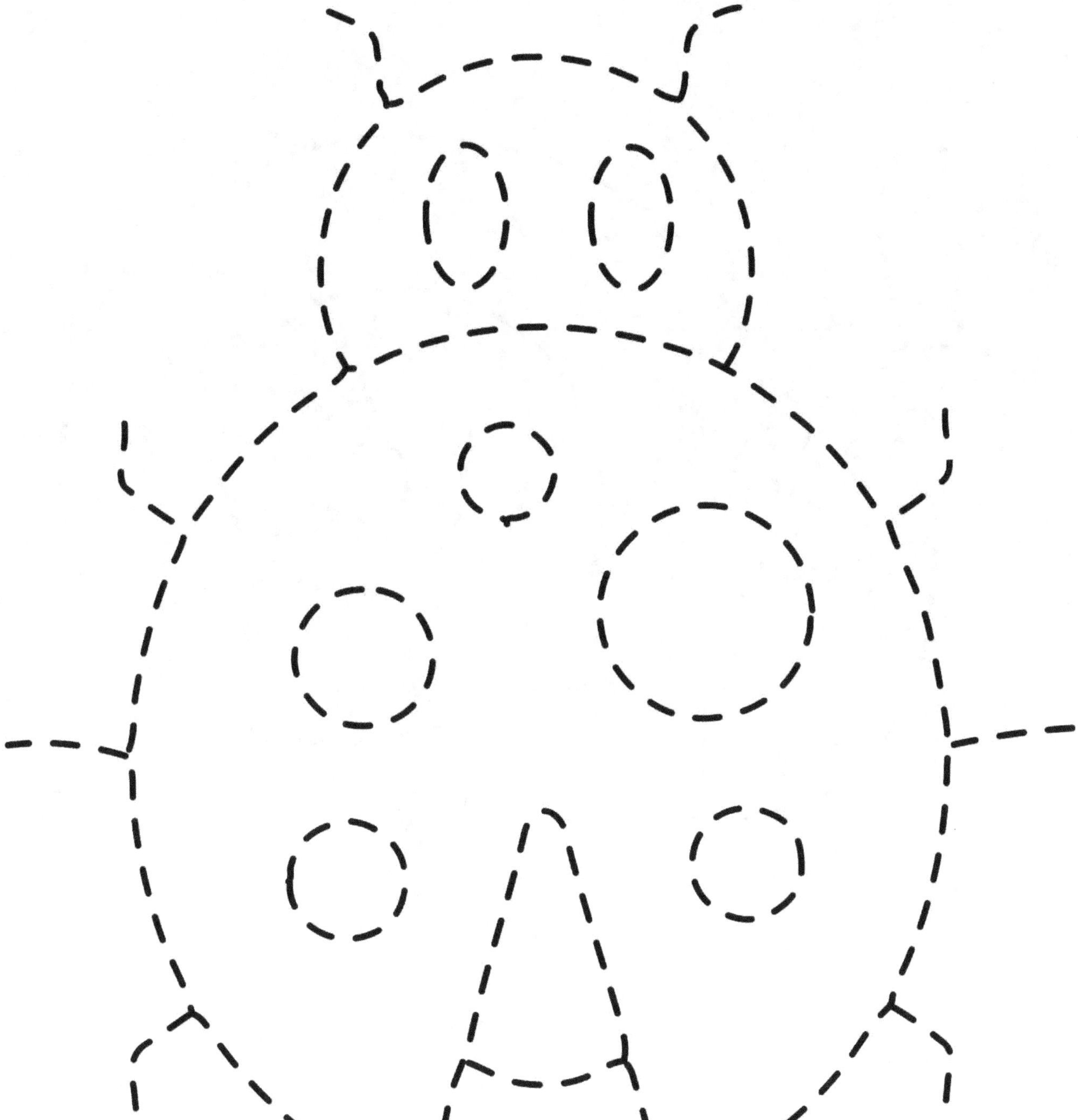

 # TRACE AND COLOR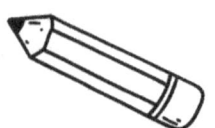

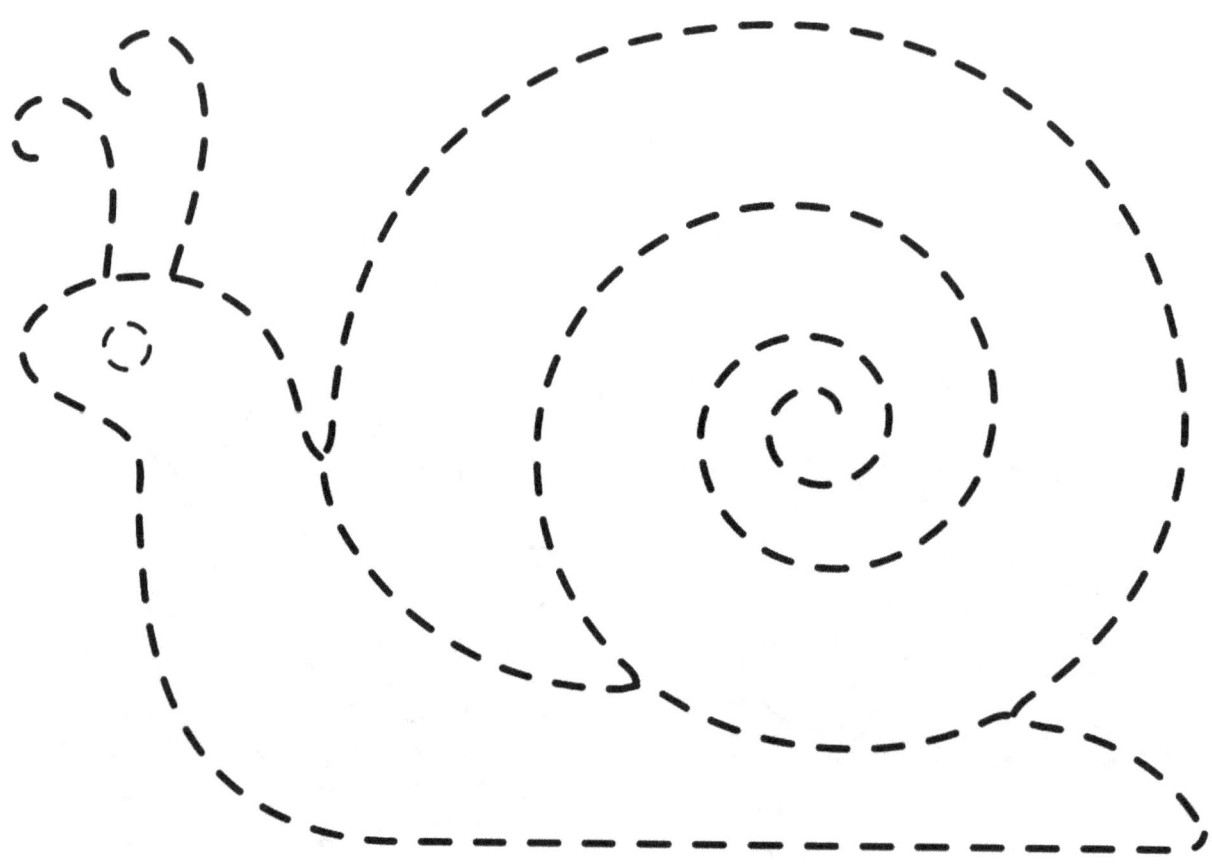

 # TRACE AND COLOR

 # TRACE AND COLOR

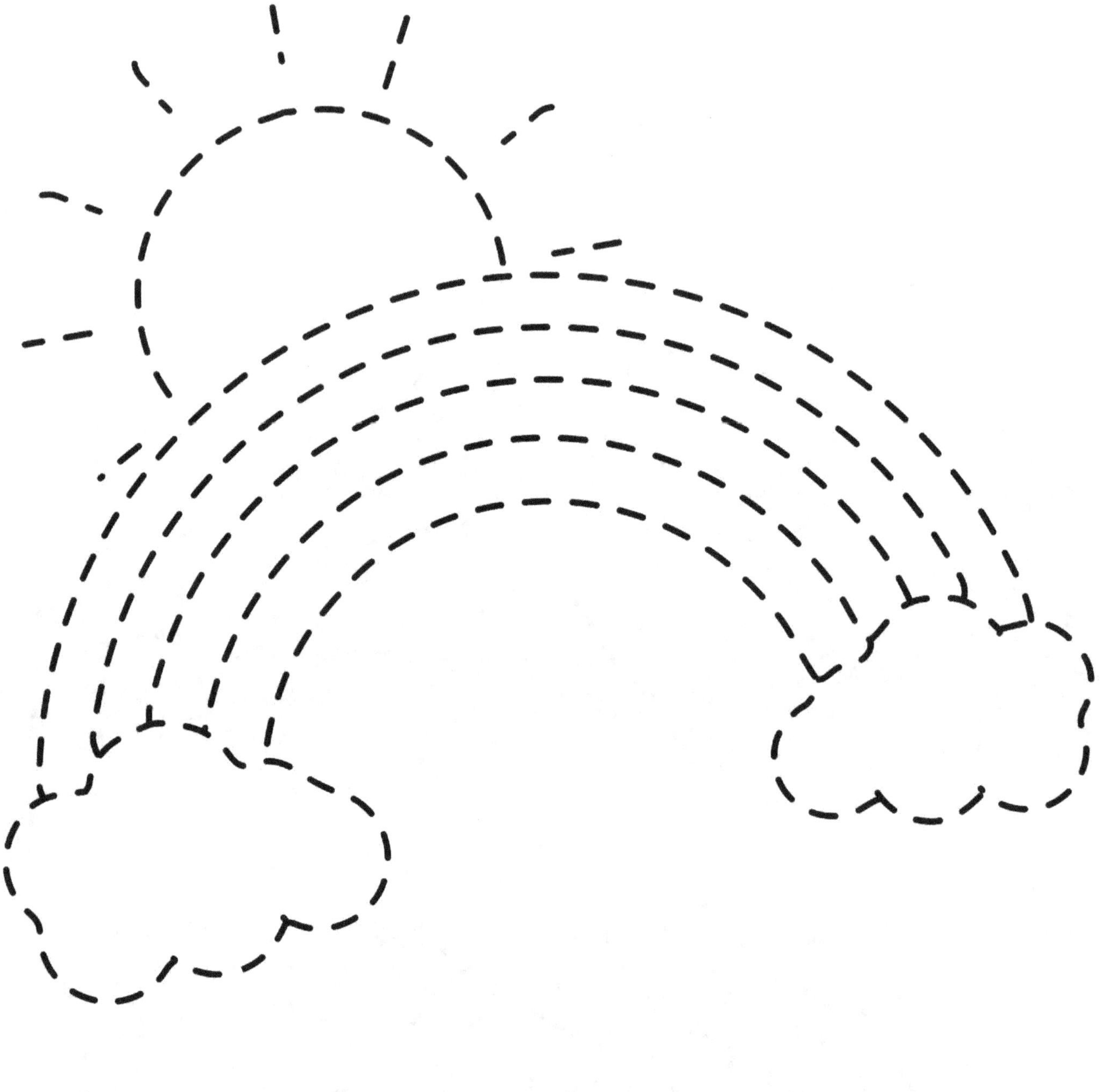

 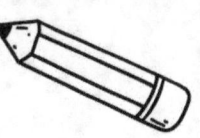

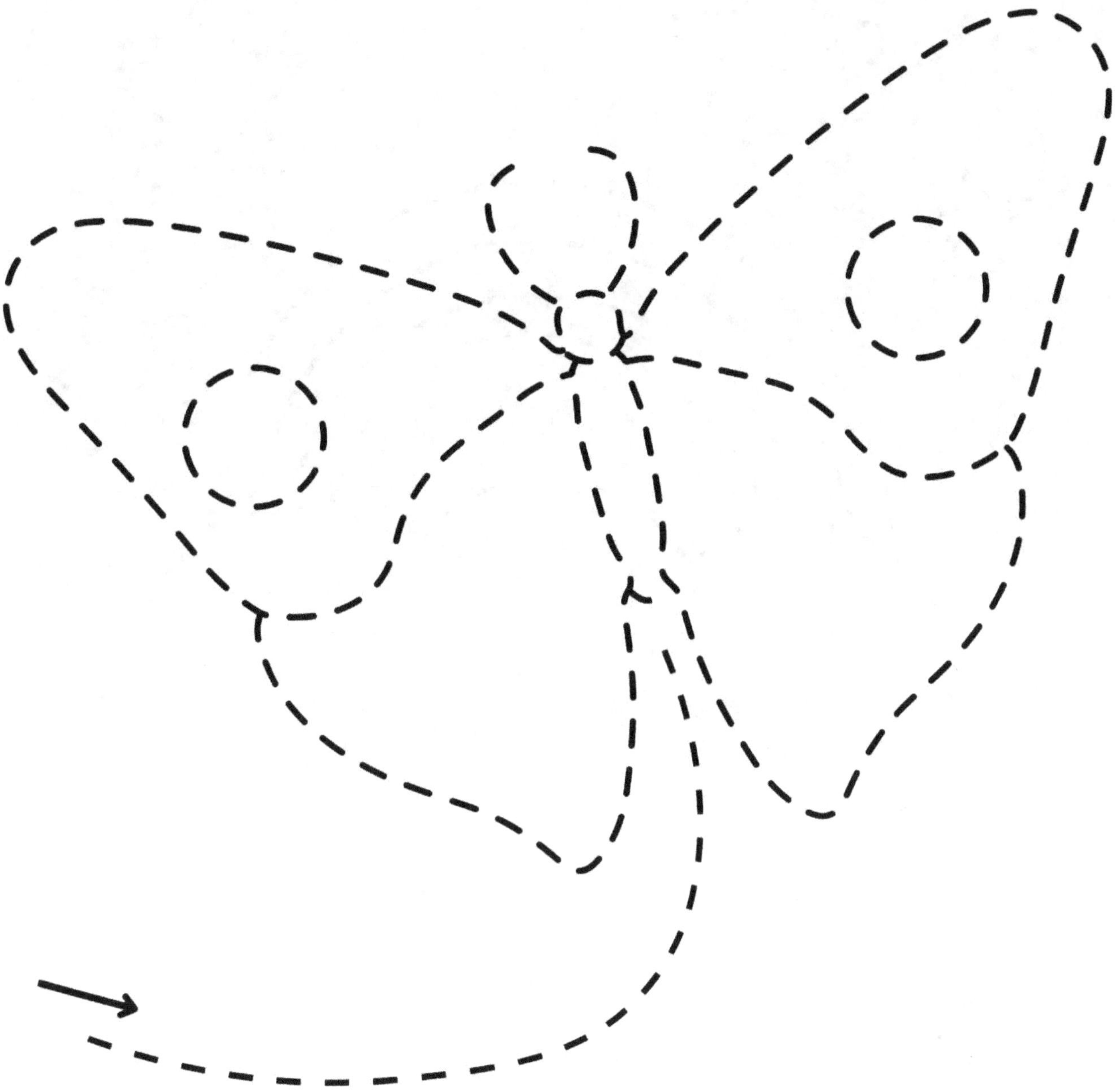

 # TRACE AND COLOR

 # TRACE AND COLOR

 # TRACE AND COLOR

 # TRACE AND COLOR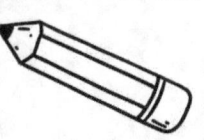

 # TRACE AND COLOR

TRACE AND COLOR

 # TRACE AND COLOR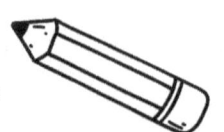

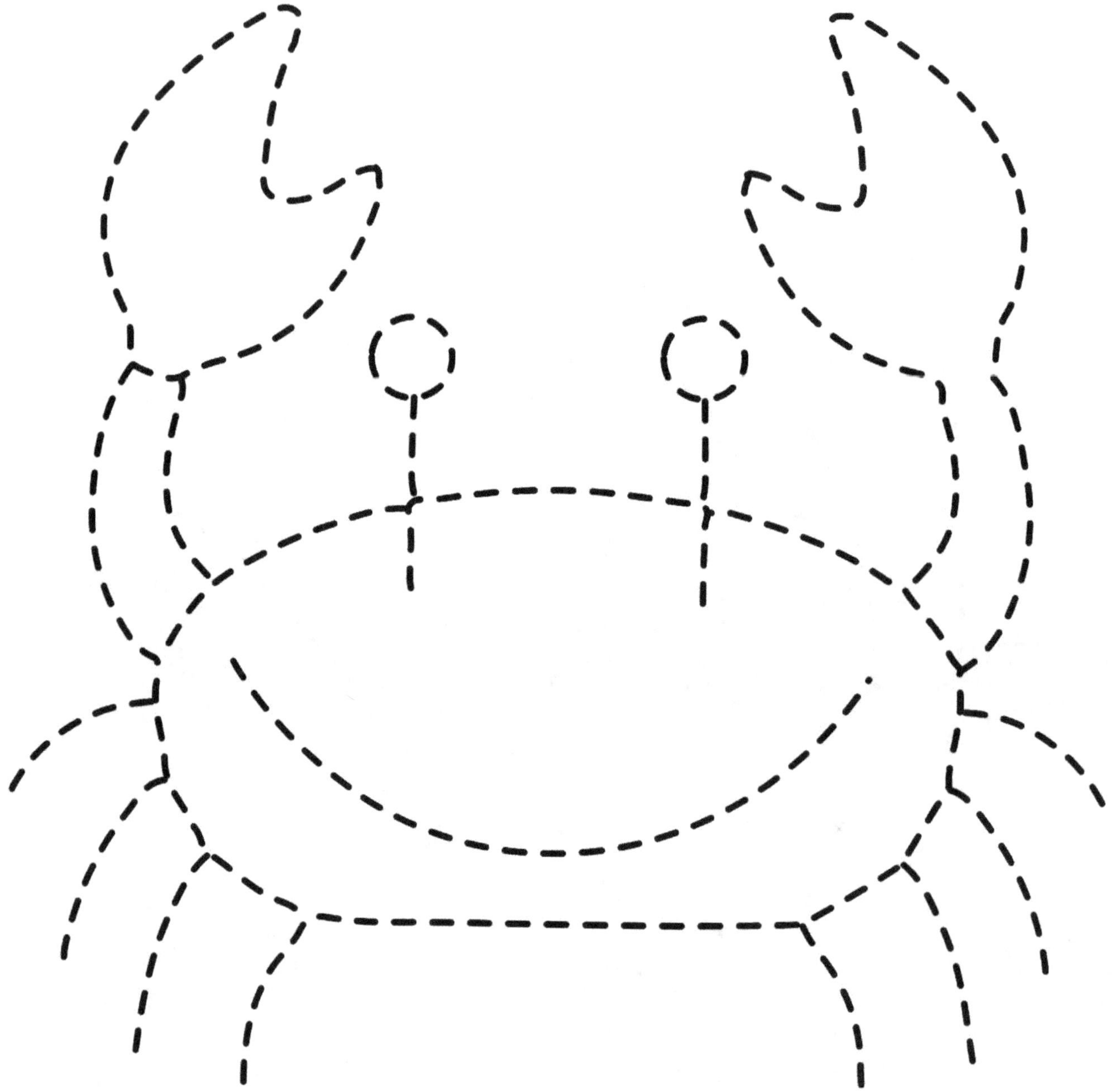

 # TRACE AND COLOR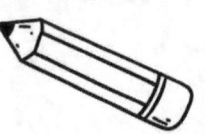

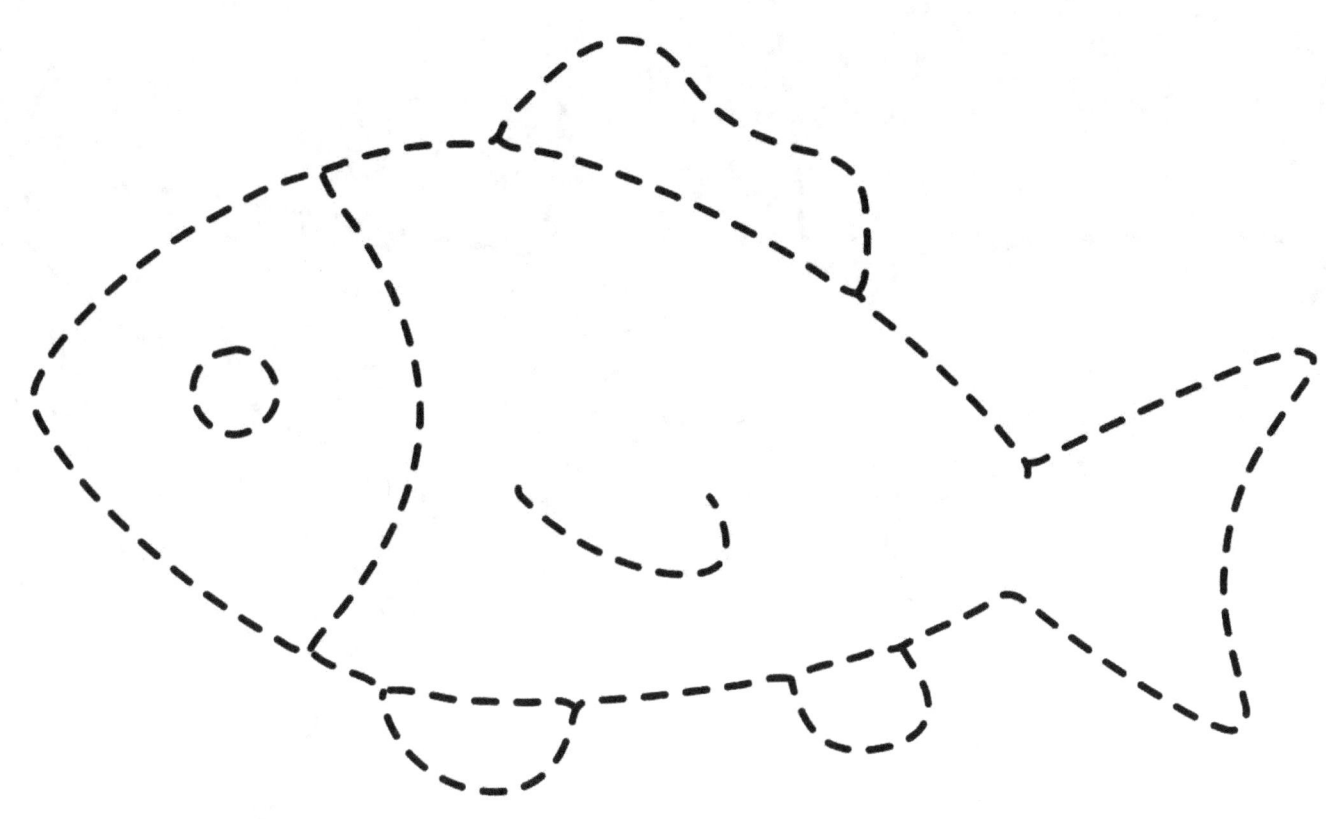

 # TRACE AND COLOR

 # TRACE AND COLOR

 # TRACE AND COLOR

 # TRACE AND COLOR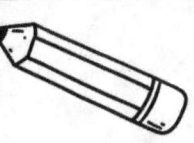

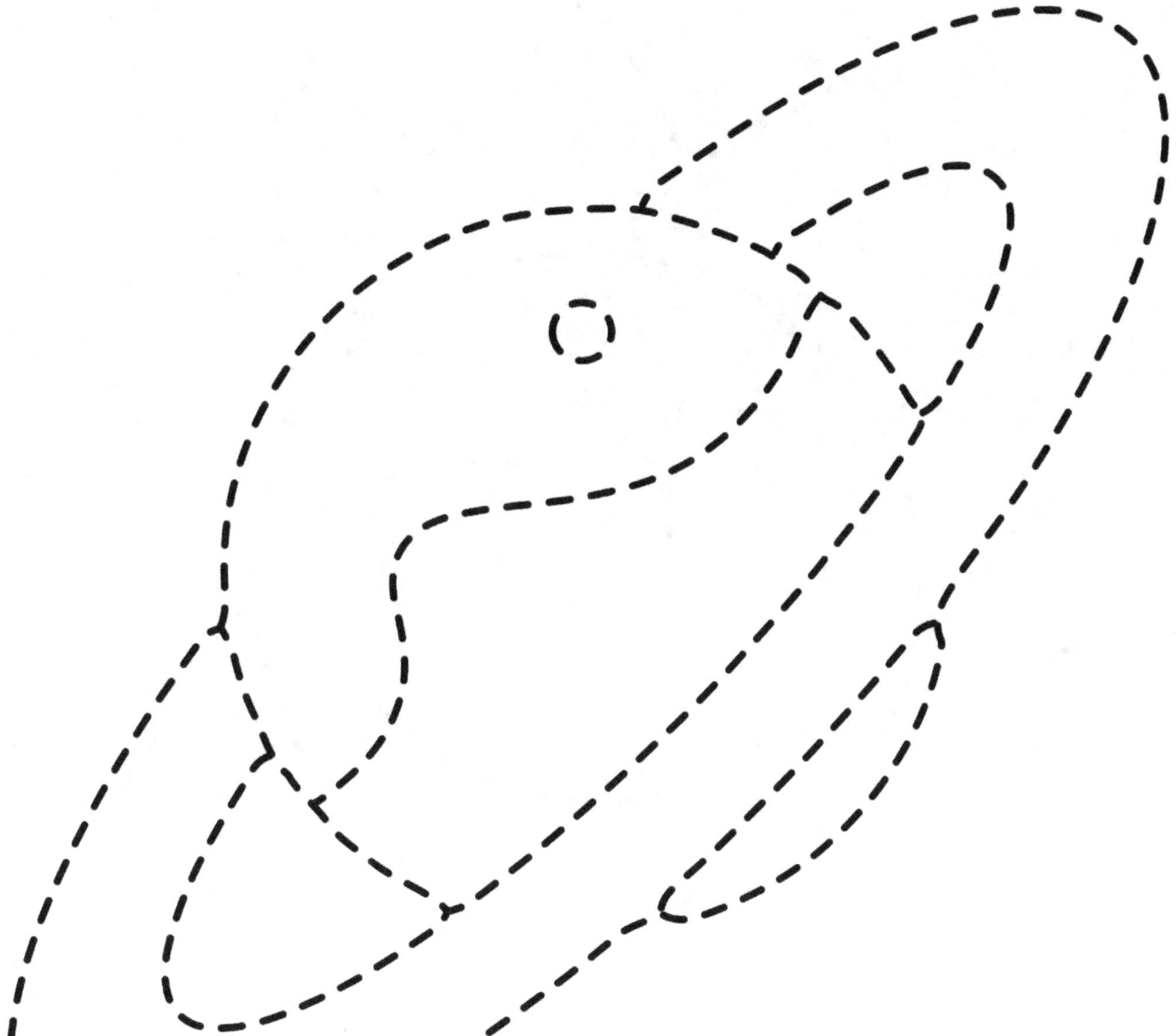

 # TRACE AND COLOR

 # TRACE AND COLOR

DOT TO DOT

Connect the dots and color the picture.

16 1

15

2

14 3

13 4

12 5

11 6

10 9 8 7

4 5

3

2 6

1 7

8

 # DOT TO DOT

Connect the dots and color the picture.

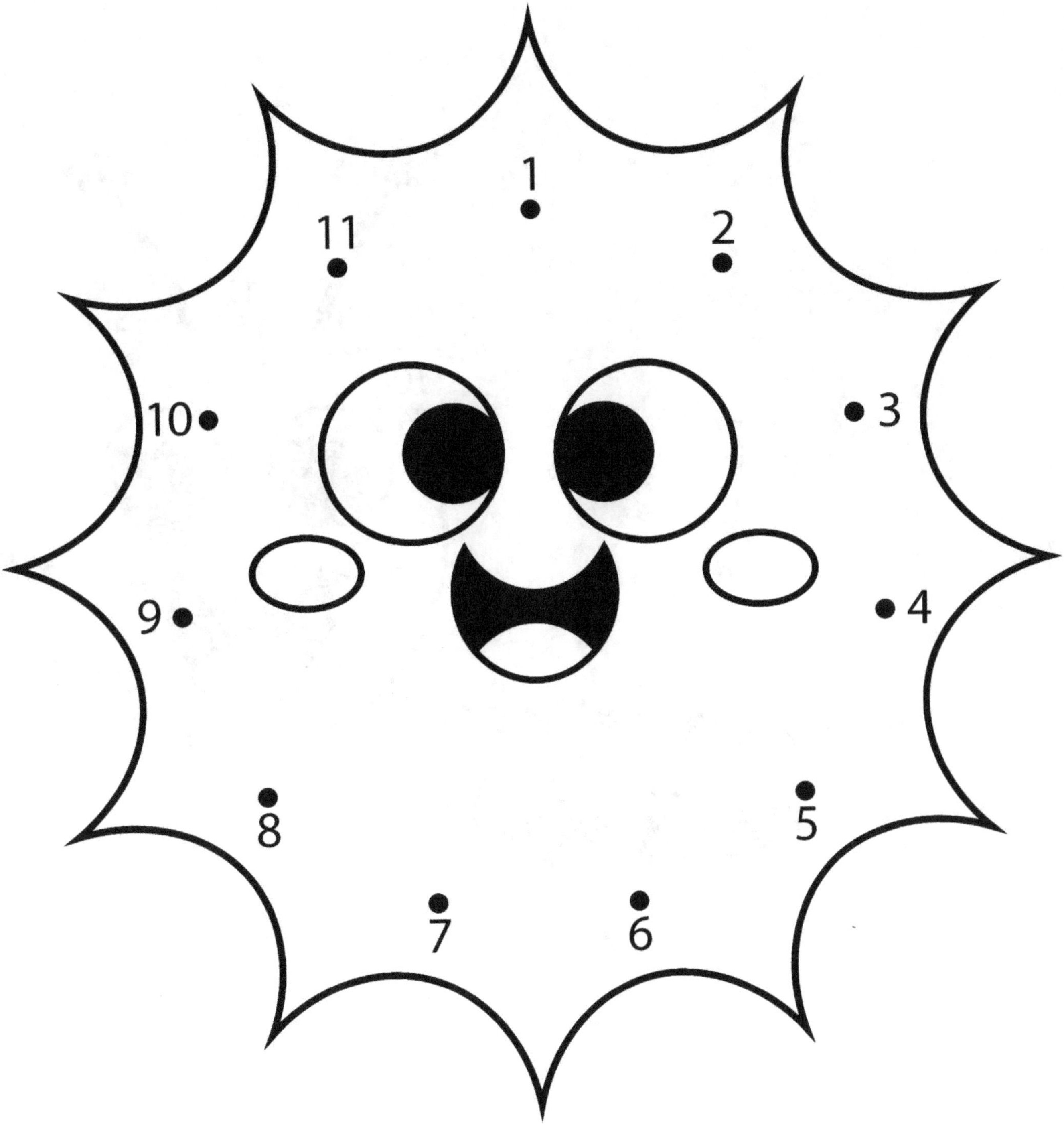

1

11

2

10

3

9

4

8

5

7   6

 # DOT TO DOT

Connect the dots and color the picture.

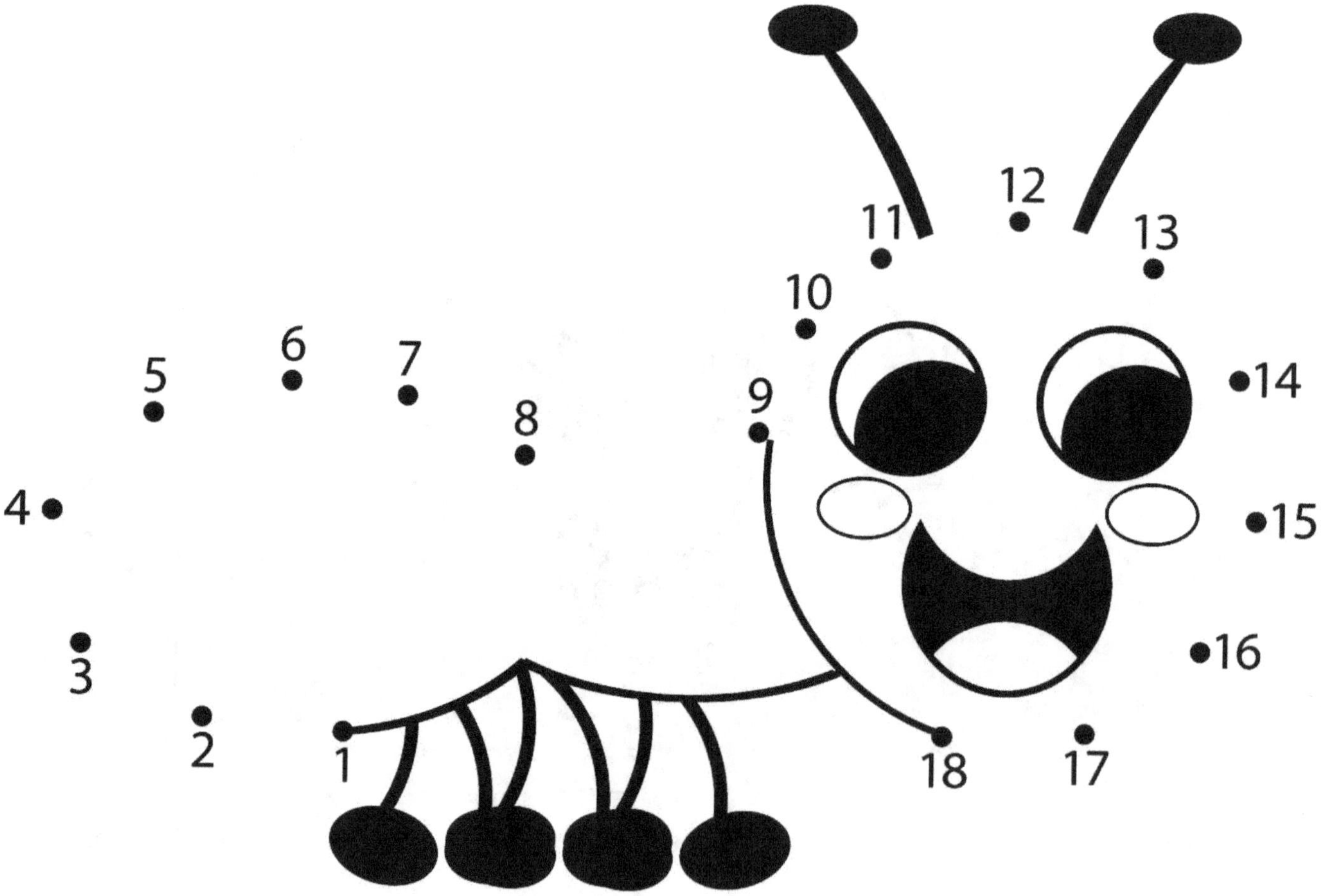

11 12 13

10

5   6   7   14

8   9

4   15

3   16

2   1   18 17

DOT TO DOT

Connect the dots and color the picture.

1

2

3

4

1

·2

5

3

7   6   ·4

8   ·5

9   6

10

 # DOT TO DOT
Connect the dots and color the picture.

4

5

7

8

3

6

9

2

1

10

11

12

 # DOT TO DOT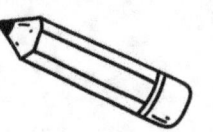
Connect the dots and color the picture.

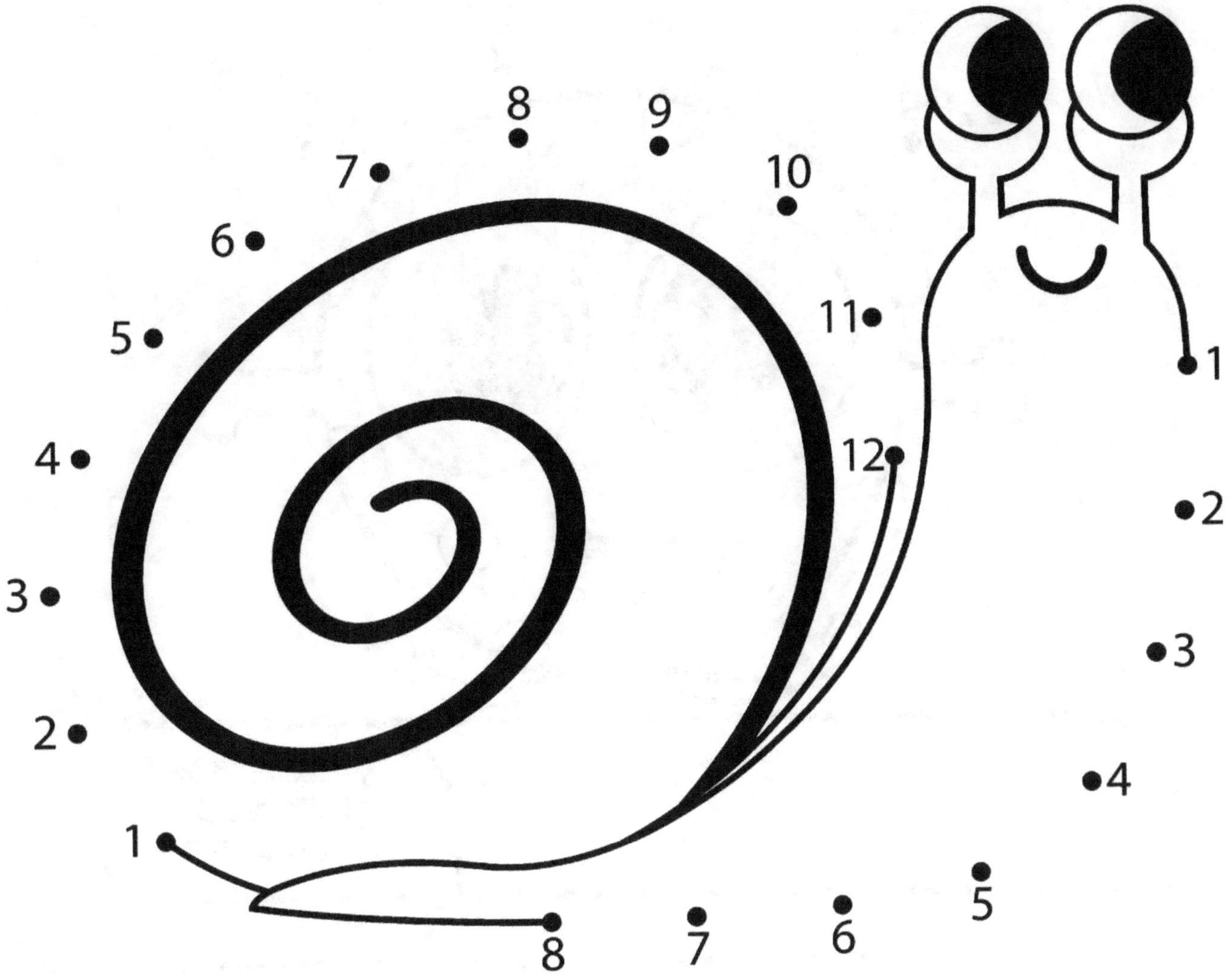

8

9

7

10

6

11

5

1

4

12

2

3

3

2

4

1

5

8   7   6

5

6

4

7

3

8

2

9

1

10

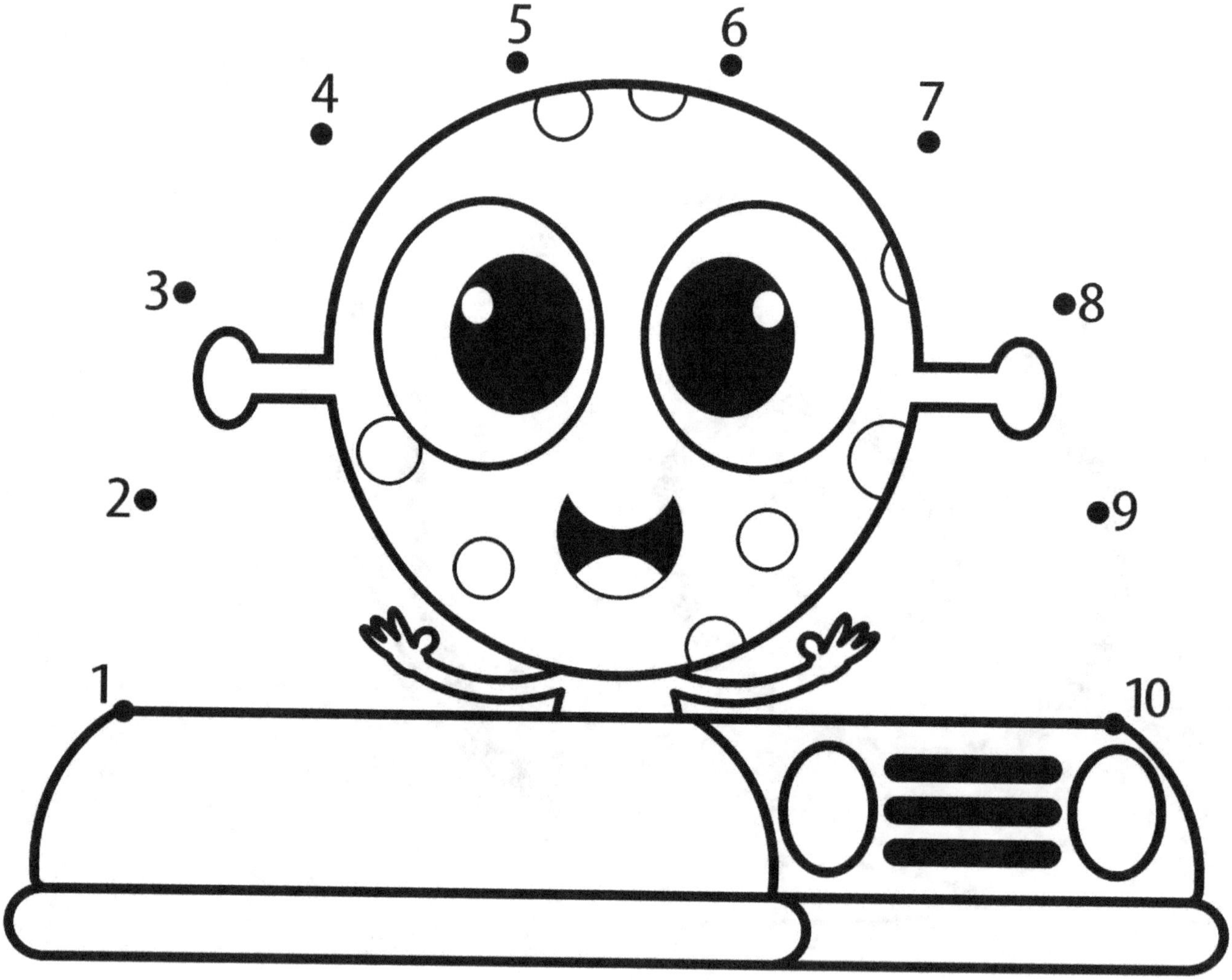

DOT TO DOT

Connect the dots and color the picture.

5
6
4
7
3
8
2
9
1
10

 # DOT TO DOT
Connect the dots and color the picture.

3 •   • 4   • 5   • 6   • 7

2 •

8 •

1 •   10 •   • 9

 # DOT TO DOT

Connect the dots and color the picture.

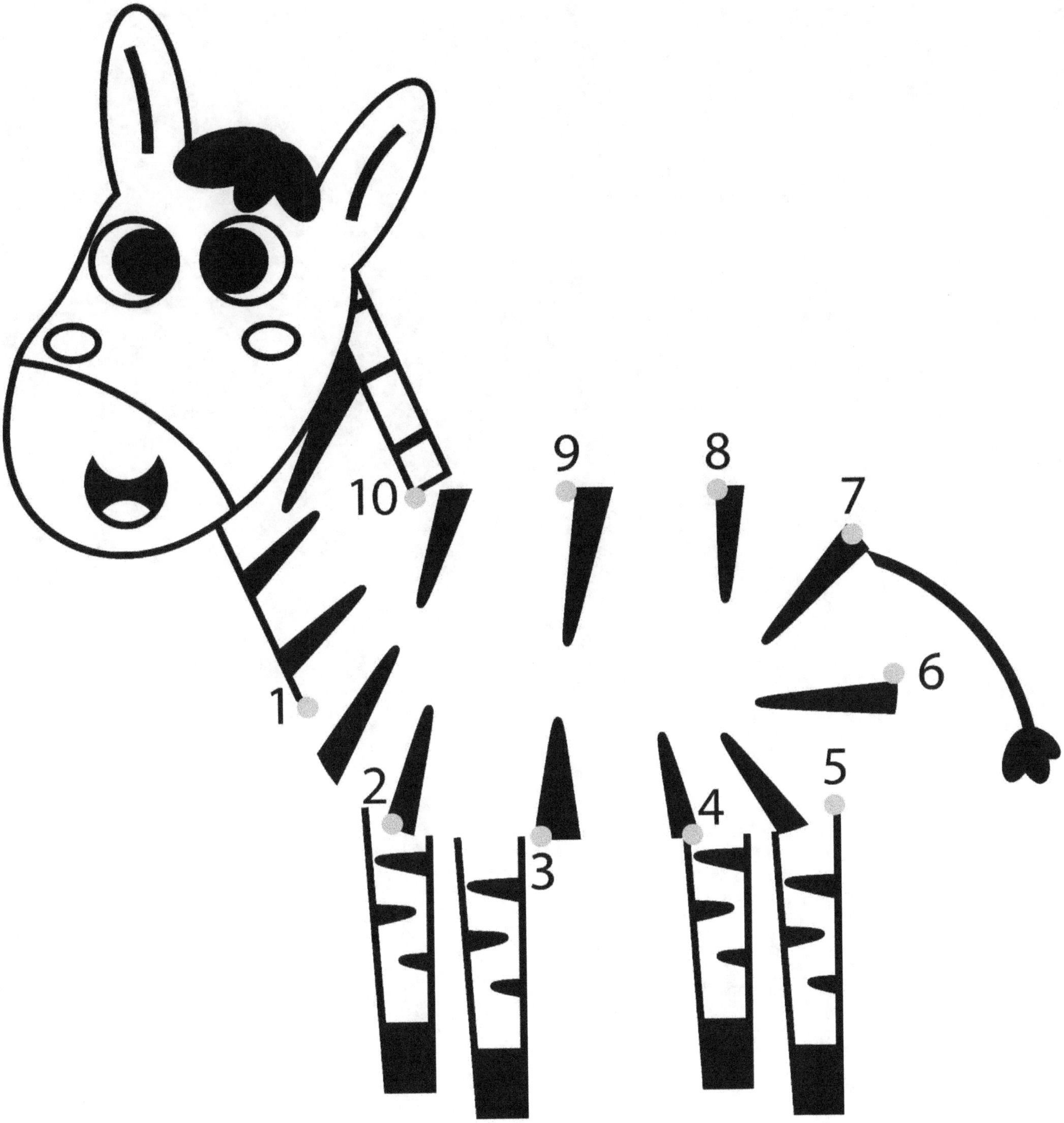

10   9   8   7

1

6

2

5

3   4